The Gospel of Judas

The Gospel of Judas

Rewriting Early Christianity

Simon Gathercole

OXFORD
UNIVERSITY PRESS

Great Clarendon Street, Oxford OX2 6DP

Oxford University Press is a department of the University of Oxford.
It furthers the University's objective of excellence in research, scholarship,
and education by publishing worldwide in

Oxford New York

Auckland Cape Town Dar es Salaam Hong Kong Karachi
Kuala Lumpur Madrid Melbourne Mexico City Nairobi
New Delhi Shanghai Taipei Toronto

With offices in

Argentina Austria Brazil Chile Czech Republic France Greece
Guatemala Hungary Italy Japan Poland Portugal Singapore
South Korea Switzerland Thailand Turkey Ukraine Vietnam

Oxford is a registered trade mark of Oxford University Press
in the UK and in certain other countries

Published in the United States
by Oxford University Press Inc., New York

British Library Cataloguing in Publication Data

Data available

Library of Congress Cataloging in Publication Data

Data available

Typeset by SPI Publisher Services, Pondicherry, India
Printed in Great Britain
on acid-free paper by
Biddles Ltd., King's Lynn, Norfolk

ISBN 978–0–19–922584–2

1 3 5 7 9 10 8 6 4 2

Contents

List of Illustrations

Introduction

WORLD EXCLUSIVE
The Gospel of Judas Iscariot
'Greatest archaeological discovery of all time'
threat to 2000 years of Christian teaching
(*Mail on Sunday*, 12 March 2006)

THE SO-CALLED 'threat to 2000 years of Christian teaching' which has attracted so much attention recently is the new take on the death of Jesus. Despite the rise of 'fish' badges on the backs of Christians' cars, the most easily identifiable Christian symbol is probably still the cross, because it is Jesus Christ's death and resurrection which have historically been the central theme of Christian teaching. As Saint Paul, one of the earliest Christians, put it: 'May I never boast except in the cross of our Lord Jesus Christ ...' (Gal. 6: 14).

There are several sets of villains in the narrative of the death of Jesus in the four New Testament Gospels. Among the Jewish opponents of Jesus, there are the crowds who call for his execution, the chief priests (the Temple hierarchy), the scribes (a leading contingent of the Pharisees, usually in rivalry with the Temple authorities), and the Herodians, adherents of Herod and his family. According to one of the Gospel writers, Herod is himself involved in the trial process. On the Roman side, there are the soldiers who callously mock Jesus and administer his execution, and Pontius Pilate, who famously washes his hands of the whole business.

But as Jesus' death is presented in the Gospels, perhaps the worst offender is one of his own disciples—Judas Iscariot. He is the one who—despite being himself a follower of Jesus—approaches the Jewish authorities and offers to hand Jesus over to them for the slave's purchase price of thirty pieces of silver. He dies an ignominious death under the divine curse, and has taken his place in Christian history as the villain *par excellence*. In Dante's *Inferno*, for example, he merits being half eaten by Satan, 'His head within, his jerking legs outside.'[1]

This traditional picture of Judas undergoes serious surgery, however, in a newly discovered manuscript from Egypt containing the *Gospel of Judas*, finally released to the public a month after the *Mail on Sunday*'s portentous announcement. In this text, which survives in the ancient Egyptian language of Coptic, Judas, far from being an infamous villain, is actually Jesus' specially chosen disciple, and the recipient of a special revelation from Jesus. This secret knowledge is far superior to anything possessed by the other disciples—in fact, it is of a different character altogether.

The theology expressed in this secret knowledge revealed to Judas reflects the influence of a system of thought in antiquity now frequently called 'Gnosticism'. This has unfortunately been a word so over-used that some scholars have wanted it to be given a decent burial. But it need not be ditched quite yet, as long as it is clear what is meant by it. Here it is used to describe a set of beliefs, held by a variety of different movements, central to which are three main ideas: (1) the world was created not by the supreme God but by a second-rate deity who—since he is either weak or evil or both—forms a world which is from the outset fallen and corruptible; (2) it is therefore essential to escape from this earthly and bodily imprisonment and have one's divine self returned to its original home in heavenly luminosity; and (3) this salvation is achieved by attaining to special 'knowledge' (the Greek for which is *gnōsis*, hence Gnosticism)—insight which is revealed only to an elite few favoured by the supreme deity. This way of looking at God and the world was already known before the publication of the *Gospel of Judas*, principally from the discovery of a hoard of manuscripts in 1945–6 near Nag Hammadi in Egypt.

Before examining the *Gospel of Judas* proper, the first chapter of this book will cover the action-packed story of the discovery of the codex (the bound papyrus volume containing the *Gospel of Judas*), as well as giving an account of its reconstruction and recent publication. The next two chapters explore the earliest portrayals of Judas and his role in the death of Jesus, covering not only the New Testament but also the pictures of Judas in the second century CE. Chapter 4 will present a fresh translation of the Coptic text of the *Gospel of Judas*, interspersed with explanatory material covering the Gnostic context, the flow of thought in the book, as well as sections of the text which are difficult to understand (which is a good proportion of them, in fact). Although the work is newly discovered, we have known of the existence of a Gospel of Judas for centuries, and Chapter 5 will examine the sources from antiquity which refer to it. The last two chapters offer some comment on the date of the work, and of its significance for our knowledge of Jesus and early Christianity. Without spoiling the ending too much, the conclusion will be that the *Gospel of Judas* ultimately does not tell us anything about Jesus that we did not already know, although it is a fascinating window onto the world of second-century Gnosticism and its conflict with 'mainstream' Christianity.

Although this book is not aimed primarily at scholars, research in the *Gospel of Judas* is so much in its infancy that any study, however modest, is bound to touch on aspects of the text which have not yet been explored. Chapter 3 here, for example, makes a new suggestion for how the *Gospel of Judas* may be related to Gnostic speculation (hitherto ignored) about Judas which was in the air at around the same time that this new Gospel was written. In addition, Chapters 5 and 6 offer contributions to the scholarly discussion about the date of the work, especially on the evidence that the *Gospel of Judas* is dependent upon one of the New Testament Gospels. These, along with the other observations scattered throughout the book, will I hope be given consideration in the scholarly discussion which will no doubt pile up in the future.[2]

The principal aim of this book, however, is to examine the central claims made both by the *Gospel of Judas* itself and by journalists and scholars on its behalf. Some, as per the *Mail on Sunday*, have presumed that simply by virtue of being an ancient document (which it undoubtedly is) the work threatens to give an account of Jesus and his betrayal by Judas more reliable than that of the New Testament. A recent documentary produced by *National Geographic* takes a similar line, to the effect that the *Gospel of Judas* may well be just as old as Matthew, Mark, Luke, and John. More commonly, however, the view is propounded that the *Gospel of Judas* joins the ranks of the four New Testament Gospels (as well as other early Christian Gospels) as a new addition to the tumultuous confusion—or, put differently, the fascinating diversity—of early Christianity and its portrayals of Jesus. A new school of thought has emerged and attracted a good deal of media attention which advances this case for a multiplicity of early Christianities, none of which should be prioritized over any other. After all, the story goes, it was only because one particular party was the victor in the early Christian power-struggle that what we now know as Christianity won the day. This new approach to Christian origins has been adopted both by some scholars and by popularizers such as Dan Brown, and now the fight is on to determine whether the *Gospel of Judas* supports this revisionist approach or not. Nor is the battle merely over the past. The aim of this book is to work out not only what the *Gospel of Judas* meant, but also whether it means anything for our understanding of the history of earliest Christianity and of Jesus today.

1

Out of Egypt

IN THE autumn of 2000, the codex containing the *Gospel of Judas* was in the hands of Bruce Ferrini, an art dealer based in Ohio. With two colleagues, he drew up an action plan for commercializing the work, and envisaged various teams—for conservation, translation, and so on, but also including a 'Team to Sensationalize and Romanticize'.[1] Ferrini's plans ultimately fell through because he had to relinquish the codex, but the *Gospel of Judas* has certainly not vanished into unsung obscurity as a result.

Almost as sensational as the contents of the document is the tale of the *Gospel of Judas*'s journey to the present—its discovery, its various travels on the wrong side of the law, its price-tags, its spell in a freezer, and the effect that it has had on those who have come into contact with it. Also fascinating is the way in which the document has recently been spun. This chapter will cover some of the highlights of the journey that the *Gospel of Judas* has undertaken in the past three decades, with a look, in addition, at how the text has been talked about in the course of its public release and thereafter.[2]

Out of Egypt

THE CODEX

To be unsensational and unromantic for a moment, we should describe what exactly it is that has been found. Some of the details of our manuscript's discovery and movements over the last thirty years are far from clear. However, at least when dealing with the physical object as we have it now we are in the realms of fairly clear realities.

The volume containing our text of the *Gospel of Judas* is a leather-bound codex of 66 pages, measuring about 16 cm × 29 cm.[3] The *Gospel of Judas* appears on pages 33–58, with the title coming at the end of the work. Before it come two other Gnostic writings: 'the Epistle of Peter to Philip', and then one called simply 'James'; the *Judas* text is followed at the end of the codex by a work about a figure called 'Allogenes'. As with almost all manuscripts from the ancient world, these are not the original editions handwritten by the authors themselves, they are copies made by later scribes. Furthermore, probably all the texts, and certainly our copy of the *Gospel of Judas*, are not only copies but copies of translations. This version of the *Gospel of Judas* survives not in the original Greek, but in Coptic.

Coptic is a language descended from ancient Egyptian but written predominantly in the Greek alphabet rather than in the famous hieroglyphs. The specific dialect has been labelled a Middle-Egyptian variety of Sahidic Coptic, reflecting the influence of where the text was found.[4] According to Coptic specialist Stephen Emmel, it is a very professional copy, and is in a style of handwriting similar to that of the manuscripts found at Nag Hammadi.[5]

Not many manuscripts go through a process of scrutiny as rigorous as that initiated by the Maecenas Foundation and National Geographic, the two organizations which have been responsible for the restoration and publication of the codex. As well as ancient historians and linguists, scientists have also been involved: the papyrus been carbon dated, and even the ink analysed. The carbon dating was overseen by Dr Timothy Jull, Director of the University of Arizona's Accelerated Mass Spectrometry facility, using samples of the pages and a small piece of the leather binding material. Jull's analysis revealed a date, to an estimated 90 per cent degree of accuracy, of 280 CE ± 60 years, in other words, a time-frame of 220–340 CE.

This was confirmed by investigation of the ink, which was carried out by a company specializing in microscopy and materials analysis: 'Transmission electron microscopy (TEM) confirmed the presence of carbon black as a major constituent of the ink, and the binding medium is a gum—which is consistent with inks from the third and fourth centuries CE.'[6] So a date for our codex in the third or fourth century is beyond reasonable doubt.

THE DISCOVERY

The shenanigans surrounding this manuscript of the *Gospel of Judas* have included a colourful cast of characters, but one on whom we have very little information is the individual who allegedly shared a resting place with the *Gospel of Judas* for a number of centuries. In fact, one version of the story goes, next to a shrouded skeleton a limestone box was found containing four codices: the codex of Gnostic works which included the

Gospel of Judas, two volumes of biblical texts, and a fourth with a mathematical treatise in Greek. Although few people would want to be considered to agree with everything on their book-shelves, the obvious implication of our man being buried with these volumes is that they were probably some of his prized pos-sessions. Presumably the man was a religious scholar, a reader of both Greek and Coptic, and interested in mathematics as well—unless he was just a rich pseudo-intellectual. But all this may in any case need to be taken with a pinch of salt—in particular, the four codices may well not all have been found together.

There are several different accounts of where exactly the manuscript's resting-place was, although the two most popular stories agree on the Al-Minya Province of Egypt, specifically on an area a little over 100 miles south of Cairo as the crow flies (see Fig. 1.1). One version of events, recounted in Herb Krosney's *The Lost Gospel*, is that the site was a cave across the Nile from Maghagha (i.e. on the east side of the Nile), in the Jebel Qarara hills. On the other hand, Stephen Emmel's report made in 1983 notes that the prospective buyers of the codices were told that the discovery was made near Beni Mazar, a village a little further south, but on the other side—the west side—of the river.[7]

The man who found the manuscripts is known (or rather his pseudonym is): 'Am Samiah', a garlic-farmer and Coptic Christian, found the texts, perhaps along with his partner Mahmoud, and our religious polymath's treasured possessions were unceremoniously swiped from him some time probably in the mid- to late 1970s. Joanna Landis, one of the sources for Herb Krosney's book, was apparently taken in 1978 to the area claimed to be the place of discovery by Am Samiah. Whether it was the right spot or not, this still establishes a *terminus ad quem* for the find—it must have been before 1978.

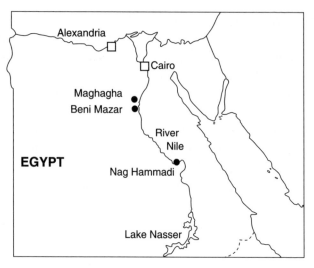

Figure 1.1. Map showing Maghagha and Beni Mazar, near which the *Gospel of Judas* was reportedly discovered.

CAIRO

Am Samiah then organized a sale to a Cairo-based dealer, 'Hanna Asabil' (another—male—pseudonym), who traded from both his apartment and his antiquities shop in Cairo. In order to maximize his profit margin on these codices, Hanna sought a wider market by going into partnership with a more experienced dealer.

Hanna had previously done business with one Nicolas Koutoulakis, a dealer based in Switzerland who was extremely well-connected in the Middle East. He was certainly able to help Hanna with selling the codices for a decent price, and yet Hanna's association with him turned out to be something of a poisoned chalice.

'Linked'—as they say in the tabloids—with Koutoulakis was a woman known variously as 'Effie', or 'Mia' (and so perhaps a Greek with a name like Evphemia, or Evthymia). She visited Hanna's apartment with some associates in March 1980 and inspected his booty with a view to buying everything in the collection. They left with a list of his inventory, promising to go to Alexandria for the necessary funds and then to return. That next day, however, disaster struck for Hanna in the shape of a very well-planned burglary on his apartment, in which he lost everything. Hanna, naturally enough, was left a broken man as a result. All roads at this point tend to lead to Effie/Mia as being the culprit, although Koutoulakis does not himself seem to have been involved. One London dealer was sold some of Hanna's inventory by her; Hanna's manuscripts were later recovered through Koutoulakis, and some loose leaves of the *Gospel of Judas* were (much later) obtained from her as well. The codices were eventually returned to Hanna in the summer of 1982 by Koutoulakis at the latter's villa in Geneva, and Hanna left them in a nearby bank vault before leaving for home.

1983: THE GENEVA HOTEL ROOM

On 15 May 1983, John Calvin would have been turning in his unmarked grave. His beloved Geneva was the location for a rather cloak-and-dagger meeting of Hanna, accompanied by the rather more effective associate he had now enlisted, and a group of scholars trying to buy the *Gospel of Judas* manuscript and the other codices. (The shady atmosphere of the meeting was no doubt partly created by the fact that the codices had now illegally left Egypt.) Three scholars had flown over from the United States to see them, and a fourth, Stephen Emmel, travelled from Rome.

But only about half an hour was allowed for them to examine the codices, with no notes or photos. What was even more disconcerting was the condition of the texts: they were being kept in shoebox-like cardboard containers. The scholarly desire to preserve was instantly awakened, but then fell the bombshell— the asking price. Hanna's demand of a cool $3 million for the codices brought an abrupt end to the negotiations.[8]

1984: THE *GOSPEL OF JUDAS* IN THE USA

The next year, 1984, was another *annus horribilis* for our manuscript. The hapless Hanna embarked on a trip to the United States to try his luck there, and was initially successful in making contacts with the Coptic community in New Jersey. This led to an attempt to sell the manuscripts to a renowned New York dealer, H. P. Kraus, but no progress was made because Kraus was intimidated by what he took to be the armed muscle accompanying Hanna (in fact, Hanna's companions were Coptic monks). A second attempt was slightly more promising: the codices were taken on 27 March 1984 to be examined by Roger Bagnall, Professor of Classics at Columbia University. By this time, Hanna had climbed down and reduced the asking price—now a mere $1 million. But this was still far too steep.

Apart from anything else, this was bad news for the manuscripts. While in New York, Hanna placed them in a bank vault in a town rejoicing in the name of Hicksville, on Long Island. The codices stayed there for sixteen years, and Long

Island is a place where—as American TV meteorologists might put it—there is 'a lot of weather'. In the course of this sixteen-year period, for example, the island was hit by Hurricane Gloria (1985), Hurricane Bob (1991), and Hurricane Floyd (in 1999). The alternation of freezing winters with the regular northeaster blizzards on the one hand, and the humidity of the summers on the other, left the codices in a fearful state. When Hanna came back in April 2000 to retrieve them, he found to his horror that parts of the papyrus were slowly rotting.

SPRING 2000: THE TCHACOS PURCHASE

A fellow-dealer has said of Frieda Tchacos that 'she speaks all the languages, and does business on the highest level; millions and millions of pounds.'[9] Born in Egypt, she also has Greek and Swiss citizenship, and studied in Switzerland and at the École du Louvre in Paris. In 1999, Tchacos received an anonymous tip-off about the manuscripts, having already followed some of their progress two decades earlier before the trail went cold. The caller sent her some photographs, and Tchacos sent these on to Yale University for identification. Sure enough, they were recognized as the codices which had been examined in Geneva in 1983.

Tchacos then pleaded with Hanna for a meeting in New York, where the manuscripts could be retrieved and a deal struck. They eventually did meet in April 2000, when a sale was agreed, but the manuscripts which changed hands were by then in terrible condition. (The price has not been revealed, but is somewhere around $300,000.)[10] In any case, Tchacos was more than compensated by a visit to Yale later in the month, soon after which came the revelation that one codex contained the *Gospel of Judas*, a fact not previously picked up.

This had a profound effect upon Tchacos. She came to believe that she had a destiny in all this, that she was 'guided by providence', commenting, 'I had a mission. Judas was asking me to do something for him. It's more than a mission, now that I think of it. I think I was chosen by Judas to rehabilitate him.'[11]

2000–2001: THE OHIO INTERLUDE

Tchacos had been hoping to sell the texts to Yale, but despite initially promising noises, the deal eventually fell through because of questions raised about where the text had been found and who the legal owner was. So in September 2000, Tchacos went to Yale to retrieve the manuscript and took it to Ohio to a dealer, Bruce Ferrini, who has become notorious as a result. Ferrini 'paid' Tchacos $2.5 million for all the manuscripts, but with post-dated cheques. We do not know much of what went on while Ferrini had the codices, but what can be deduced does not make happy reading. For one thing, almost 200 photographs (most of very poor quality) were taken of the manuscripts, and were sent to Coptic scholar Charles Hedrick. He had been led to believe that six of the good-quality photos he had received were of the *Gospel of Judas*: in fact, only one was. Hedrick transcribed and translated these pages (see Fig. 1.2), which were then somehow obtained by the irrepressible Michel van Rijn, and published on his 'artnews' website as sections of the *Gospel of Judas*.[12]

While Ferrini was organizing the team for commercializing the *Gospel of Judas*, it appears that the manuscript spent some

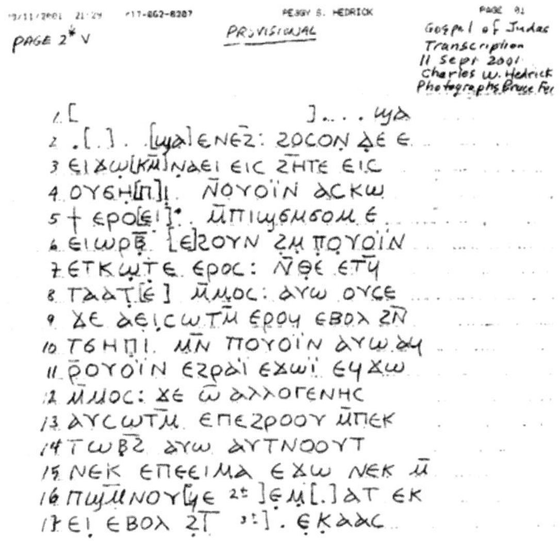

Figure 1.2. A faxed page from Charles Hedrick's transcription of what had been thought (wrongly) to be from the *Gospel of Judas*. (*The text at the top right-hand corner, dated 11 Sept. 2001, indicates Hedrick's name and that of Bruce Ferrini.*)

time in a freezer—not the ideal habitat for papyrus. Rodolphe Kasser gives a good description of the effects of this:

This inauspicious freezing apparently produced the partial destruction of the sap holding the fibers of the papyrus together, making it significantly more fragile ... Furthermore, this freezing made all the water in the papyrus migrate toward the surface of the papyrus before evaporation, bringing with it quantities of pigment from inside the fibers, which darkened many pages of the papyrus and therefore made the writing extremely difficult to read.[13]

Although it was becoming clear that the sale was not going to go through, Ferrini nevertheless hung on to the manuscript, and

Mario Roberty, Frieda Tchacos's lawyer, urged her to retrieve the manuscripts as quickly as possible. Ferrini eventually lowered his ambitions and offered Tchacos $300,000 for the mathematical work and the Epistles of Paul. In the end, Ferrini only purchased the mathematical treatise, for $100,000, and promptly broke the manuscript up and sold the pieces. The codex containing the *Gospel of Judas* was in almost as bad condition by the time it was returned to Tchacos in February 2001, and even then, the fateful date of Charles Hedrick's transcriptions (see above) implies that Ferrini had held onto his photographs. Finally, Tchacos entrusted it to Mario Roberty's Maecenas Foundation for Ancient Art, an organization based in Basle.

2001–2004: RESTORATION AND TRANSLATION

When the manuscript came to Switzerland, the man who was on hand there to work on it was the internationally renowned Coptologist, Rodolphe Kasser: he first met with Frieda Tchacos and Mario Roberty on 24 July 2001. But when Kasser first saw the text, he commented that he had never seen a manuscript in such a state: 'In the course of my long career, I have had before my eyes lots of Coptic or Greek documents on papyrus, but I have never seen one as degraded as this one'.[14] The task of deciphering the manuscript clearly needed much more than a Coptic-language specialist. Enter Florence Darbre, both a trained Egyptologist and expert papyrus conservator. She was to work with Kasser on the manuscript, and between them they carried out the staggeringly impressive task of putting it back together again. Kasser comments, in his account of the process, on 'the expertise and dexterity that was put into this operation of incomparable difficulty and gentleness by Florence Darbre...With her fairy's fingers, she made largely possible what, at first glance, appeared doomed to failure.'[15] They worked together once a month for three years in Darbre's laboratory/studio in Nyon in Switzerland, Kasser working on possible ways to place the fragments on the basis of the sense of the text, and Darbre assessing these placements from the material evidence of the fibres in the papyrus. Historian Gregor Wurst also played a role in this, by designing a computer program to help with recognizing the paths of these fibres.[16]

But despite the technical genius of the two protagonists in this process, it appears to have been more for them than a mere academic activity. We have seen the apparent effect that owning the *Gospel of Judas* codex had on Frieda Tchacos, but even Kasser and Darbre apparently did not escape some measure of a numinous tingle in their contact with the manuscript. In Kasser's announcement, at the 2004 International Association for Coptic Studies Congress, of the forthcoming publication of the *Gospel of Judas*, he commented on the survival of the text: 'It is a miracle—this word is not an exaggeration'. He then went on to talk wistfully about his own role in the drama:

The Ancients, who knew what they were talking about, used to say that Destiny—*Moira* in Greek—is 'weaved' together, fibre by fibre; likewise, human destiny, where paths cross each other unexpectedly and are built fibre by fibre. In an entirely unexpected way, quite unplanned, human destinies crossed paths. This is what happened in Switzerland a few years ago.[17]

Florence Darbre also said that she was 'spiritually in accord' with the document, although she may merely be referring to the work having gone smoothly and the experience of reconstructing the manuscript being a happy one.[18]

After Kasser's painstaking work on the reconstruction of the text, to produce a translation of it would probably have been a relatively easy task. Although Kasser was the driving force behind the translation by virtue of his linguistic expertise and the enormous amount of time he had already spent with the manuscript, Stephen Emmel and Marvin Meyer also collaborated on the English version.[19]

'MONOPOLISTS' V. 'WHISTLEBLOWERS'

All this has been carried out under the auspices of the Maecenas Foundation, to which Kasser pays enthusiastic tribute: 'It would be unjust to pass over the enormous debt of recognition that the scientific community owes Maecenas.'[20] Others have been rather less congratulatory, however.

Professor James Robinson is best known as the organizer of the international team which edited and translated the Coptic codices discovered near Nag Hammadi in 1945–6. To tie in with the public release of the *Gospel of Judas*, he published his own book, *The Secrets of Judas*, the title of which no doubt has a double meaning. The mysterious content of the *Gospel of Judas*, which has the word 'secret' in the opening sentence, is probably not the real reason for the title; for Robinson, the greater concern is the secrecy which has surrounded the process of its publication. He quotes the following memorandum sent from the Maecenas Foundation in 2000:

It is clearly understood by all persons involved that nobody, not even Bruce [Ferrini] and Frieda [Tchacos], but only the Foundation, will have the right to promulgate and commercialize any knowledge regarding, concerning or deriving from the manuscripts. Moreover, for the time being and until all legal aspects are clarified, it is in the best interest of the Project to maintain utmost secrecy about its existence.[21]

This is a red rag to a bull for someone like Robinson because of—from his point of view—its lethal cocktail of strict secrecy and absolute monopoly. He goes on to complain how all the experts involved in the project were required to put their signatures to a document swearing them to silence, and is particularly frustrated, apparently, at not being able to get information from one of his former students, Marvin Meyer. Nevertheless, Robinson eventually felt able to claim the credit for spilling the *Gospel of Judas*'s beans:

The cloak of secrecy surrounding the discovery and publication of *The Gospel of Judas* seems to have prevailed, until it was more formally broken by me, in a presentation at the annual meeting of the Society of Biblical Literature in Philadelphia on 20 November 2005.[22]

But by comparison with the other thorn in the side of the Maecenas Foundation, Robinson has been almost friendly.

Michel van Rijn boasts on his website of a Scotland Yard officer's verdict on him: 'He is involved in 90% of all cases of art smuggling throughout the world and he would gladly like to claim that he was also involved in the remaining 10%.' In the case of the *Gospel of Judas*, van Rijn has particularly championed the cause of the return of the manuscript to its rightful home in Egypt, and both Tchacos and the Maecenas Foundation have come under fire from him. He has accused Tchacos of looting from Egypt and of being a dealer for Tarek El-Sweissi, an Egyptian official serving a thirty-year prison sentence for smuggling antiquities out of the country.[23] As for the Maecenas Foundation, one journalist has compared Michel van Rijn and Mario Roberty to Professor Moriarty and Sherlock Holmes.[24] Whether or not van Rijn really did shame the Maecenas Foundation into promising to return the manuscript to Egypt, as he claims, the manuscript is now destined for the Coptic Museum in Cairo.[25]

It may be easy to criticize the Maecenas Foundation, but the fact remains that they brought in consummate professionals (such as Kasser and Darbre) to work on the text, and that everything has in fact been done very efficiently. Some have complained that the *Gospel of Judas* has been an awfully long time in appearing, and wonder how it could take three to five years to assemble, translate, and publish a relatively short text. In fact, however, for a team of people each of whom would already have numerous other projects on the go, five years is not such a long time for a reconstruction of this complexity.[26] It is also not unreasonable for Maecenas to want to recoup some of the expenses incurred in acquiring the manuscript.

2006: TO SENSATIONALIZE AND ROMANTICIZE...

The next stage in the journey is from the Maecenas Foundation to the National Geographic Society, although the latter had in fact already been involved while the reconstruction and translation were underway. According to Mario Roberty, it is currently the case that 'the Foundation owns the copyright of the Coptic text of the GoJ but we have assigned these rights exclusively to the National Geographic Society in Washington D.C.'[27] The sum of $1 million is one figure which has circulated as the amount paid by National Geographic to Maecenas for the rights to reproduce the text.

National Geographic then launched an energetic campaign to bring the *Gospel of Judas* into the public eye. On 6 April 2006, a press conference was held, and on the same day, two books published by National Geographic were launched. Herb Krosney wrote the journalistic account of the discovery of the codex with some discussion of the content of the document, and the second book was a translation of the text, with scholarly essays on the text's interpretation and historical origins by Rodolphe Kasser and others.

Both of these volumes spent weeks in the *New York Times* bestsellers' list, but the real food for popular consumption came in the form of the National Geographic TV channel's docudrama, first shown on Sunday, 9 April 2006.[28] The programme tells a good deal of the story of the discovery recounted in Krosney's book (Krosney is credited as 'co-producer' and 'research consultant and story development') and features a number of those who participated in the restoration and translation. All the hot topics are addressed in the documentary: Judas and anti-Semitism, the persecutions at the time of Irenaeus (cue gore and violence), and the Gnostics and their alternative understanding of Christianity. But it focuses predominantly on whether the *Gospel of Judas* manuscript is real or fake, in the sense of being a genuinely ancient document or a modern forgery. The carbon dating receives particular attention, and confirms the work as 'authentic'. What is only very briefly addressed, however, is the question of whether the work is in any sense historically accurate: there are brief comments by Craig Evans ('it tells us nothing about the historical Jesus or Judas') and Elaine Pagels ('how does he know that?') and we are told ultimately that it is impossible to know when the work was originally written, the implication being that it may be just as old and reliable as the New Testament Gospels. This is reinforced by the way in which the dialogues of Jesus with Judas and the other disciples are all—as in Mel Gibson's *Passion of the Christ*—translated back into Aramaic in the dramatic reconstructions. All this attempts to create the impression that the *Gospel of Judas* may be historically authentic—authentic in the sense of being reliable in its portrayal of Jesus. This position, of which Elaine Pagels is the only supporter in the programme, is one which we will see is completely implausible.

In Herb Krosney's *The Lost Gospel*, one of the two books published by National Geographic, the hyping of the *Gospel of Judas* at the expense of the work following it in the codex is particularly strong. This 'Allogenes' text is dismissed by Krosney as: 'incomprehensible, full of obscure Coptic allusions to Gnostic levels of heaven, to Allogenes and people of a different race'.[29] On the other hand, the *Gospel of Judas* is, Krosney maintains, 'a biblical account. Its message was one of faith and belief. The fresh and innovative narrative, with a revolutionary message, had survived the journey across time. That in itself was a minor miracle'.[30] This is rather a tendentious comparison, to say the least. In fact, *Allogenes* is no more (or less) 'incomprehensible' than the *Gospel of Judas*. Just as much of *Allogenes*—if not more—is concerned with stories about Jesus. As for being 'full of obscure Coptic allusions to Gnostic levels of heaven', exactly the same is true, again: *Allogenes* frequently refers to the heavenly 'aeons'—which are mentioned eighteen times in the *Gospel of Judas*. The *Gospel of Judas* does not mention 'Allogenes and people of a different race', but it does mention 'Autogenes' and people of a different race. Perhaps that makes all the difference.

In the course of this discussion, Krosney draws the following conclusion: 'This scriptural text could shatter some of the interpretations, even the foundations, of faith throughout the Christian world. It was not a novel. It was a real gospel straight from the world of early Christianity.'[31] This contention, in very much the same spirit as the documentary and other media hype, will be scrutinized in the chapters to follow.

2

Judas in the New Testament

THE LIFE of Jesus was probably first cast in book form while the infamous Nero was Roman Emperor (54–68 CE). As the generation of Jesus' immediate contemporaries was beginning to die out, the survivors turned to producing numerous accounts of his life, teaching, death, and resurrection: by the time Luke begins writing his Gospel, he reports that 'many' had done so already (Luke 1: 1). And integral to each of the four earliest surviving accounts of Jesus' life and death is the part played in it all by Judas Iscariot.

This much is evident in the *Gospel of Judas* as well, although the relationship between Jesus and Judas there undergoes a radical change. This chapter and the next, though, will hold back from discussing the *Gospel of Judas* at this stage, and will instead explore the other accounts of Jesus and Judas up to the end of the second century CE. Here we will focus on how Judas fares in the New Testament. The Gospels of Matthew, Mark, Luke, and John (along with the book of Acts) not only provide us with the earliest evidence for Judas (a point which will be justified later), but also form the basis for the Christian Church's understanding of Jesus' betrayal and death on the cross.

Judas in the New Testament

'JUDAS, CALLED ISCARIOT'

Much of Judas Iscariot's background still remains a mystery. 'Judas' is the Greek spelling of 'Judah' (in Hebrew, *Yehudah*), and would have been the name given to him by his father Simon Iscariot (John 6: 71; 13: 2, 26). The original Judah in the book of Genesis was a son of Jacob, one of the great patriarchs of the nation of Israel, and the territory around Jerusalem (Judah, and later *Judaea*) was named after him. This made the name very popular for male Jews, even more so after the great second-century BCE Jewish hero Judas Maccabeus (later the subject of an oratorio by Handel). The name also gave rise to a feminine form—Judith.

The meaning of 'Iscariot' is rather more elusive: one recent book lists ten explanations that have been offered for its meaning.[1] Some have proposed that the name *Iskariotēs* or *Iskarioth* in the Gospels originally had the sense of 'assassin'— somewhat unlikely as a family name. Others argue that it means 'man of the city', the city being Jerusalem, but much more probable is 'man of Kerioth'. There was a city of Kerioth in Moab, mentioned both in the Old Testament and in the Moabite Stone. But the more likely site is the Old Testament city of Kerioth-Hezron in the extreme south of Judah, near to the southern tip of the Dead Sea (Josh. 15: 25). In any case, none of this gives much indication of Judas's real place of origin. Since the name had been in the family for at least a generation before Judas, it would almost certainly mean that his father did not actually live there— otherwise being formally named after the place would be redundant.

THE NEW TESTAMENT DOCUMENTS

The first mentions of Judas in the New Testament Gospels come in the lists there of Jesus' disciples. It is perhaps not difficult to guess which position in these lists Judas will occupy:

Matthew's Gospel	*Mark's Gospel*	*Luke's Gospel*
The names of the twelve apostles are these: first, Simon, who is called Peter, and Andrew his brother, and James the son of Zebedee, and John his brother; Philip and Bartholomew; Thomas and Matthew the tax collector; James the son of Alphaeus, and Thaddaeus; Simon the Cananaean, and Judas Iscariot, the one who handed him over. (Matt. 10: 2–4)	He appointed the twelve: Peter (the name he gave to Simon); James the son of Zebedee and John the brother of James (to both of whom he gave the name Boanerges, that is, 'sons of thunder'); Andrew, and Philip, and Bartholomew, and Matthew, and Thomas, and James the son of Alphaeus, and Thaddaeus, and Simon the Cananaean, and Judas Iscariot, who handed him over. (Mark 3: 16–19)	And when day came, he called his disciples and chose from them twelve, whom he named apostles: Simon, whom he also named Peter, and Andrew his brother, and James and John, and Philip, and Bartholomew, and Matthew, and Thomas, and James the son of Alphaeus, and Simon who was called the Zealot, and Judas the son of James, and Judas Iscariot, who became the betrayer. (Luke 6: 13–16)

So there is some variation as to the position occupied by some of the disciples: the apostles Matthew and Thomas jostle with one another; Matthew's and Luke's Gospels promote Andrew up the order to be next to his brother Simon Peter. But none of the Gospels gives Judas Iscariot any room for manoeuvre.[2]

Judas in the New Testament

Mark's Gospel

In the time of Jesus and Judas in the 20s and 30s CE, Jerusalem was probably the fourth-largest city in the Roman Empire, with—to take a rough estimate—a population of between 50,000 and 100,000. But at the time of Passover, the festival in the Jewish calendar which celebrated Israel's escape from Egypt, that population would have multiplied dramatically. Some scholars even imagine up to a million residents and pilgrims in the city in total.

Mark's Gospel, the earliest surviving account of Jesus' ministry (from perhaps the 60s CE), already has the basic elements of Judas's role in place. This first Gospel begins with Jesus' baptism and the immediate consequences of his early ministry, the conflict generated between himself and the Jewish authorities. Jesus' confrontations with powers both spiritual and political quickly led to a plot to bring about his death: 'The Pharisees went out and immediately plotted with the Herodians about how to kill him' (Mark 3: 6).

The crucial events are set in motion two days before Passover—the very time when this throng of pilgrims was swarming into the city. This indication of the date is doubly significant because, as we will see, the *Gospel of Judas* claims that the revelations in it took place in the week leading up to the third day before Passover. Mark reports that the priests and the teachers of the Law were looking to arrest Jesus surreptitiously; Judas takes the initiative, however, in going to the priests, and after some money is promised, Judas plans a way to hand Jesus over to them (Mark 14: 10–11). When the Passover preparations have been made, the disciples are just about to start eating when Jesus declares that he knows one of them at the table will hand him over, and that although this act is predestined, it would have been better for the disciple concerned if he had never been born (Mark 14: 18–21). At some point, Judas slips out and much later rejoins Jesus at the Garden of Gethsemane, this time with an armed band:

Just as Jesus was speaking, Judas, one of the twelve, came. With him was a crowd armed with swords and clubs, sent from the chief priests, the scribes and the elders. Now the 'betrayer' had agreed a sign with them: 'The one I kiss is the man; arrest him and take him away securely.' Going at once to Jesus, Judas said, 'Rabbi!' and kissed him. The men took Jesus and arrested him. (Mark 14: 43–6)

Judas, then, is strikingly emphasized in the very midst of his infamous deed as 'one of the Twelve', and still addresses Jesus as 'Rabbi'.

According to Mark, Jesus had known all along that arrest and execution were part of his destiny. In the middle of the Gospel's narrative, which is already heading rapidly towards Jesus' trial and execution, he predicts his destiny three times:

And he began to teach them that the Son of Man must suffer many things and be rejected by the elders and the chief priests and the scribes and be killed, and after three days rise again. (Mark 8: 31)

For he was teaching his disciples, saying to them, 'The Son of Man is to be handed over to men, and they will kill him. And when he is killed, after three days he will rise.' (Mark 9: 31)

'For even the Son of Man came not to be served but to serve, and to give his life as a ransom for many.' (Mark 10: 45)

Like the philosopher Socrates 400 years earlier, Jesus refuses any options of escape which may have been open to him, and goes willingly to his death. Unlike Socrates, however, Jesus does not regard his death merely as a tragedy which nevertheless leads to the release of the soul into a kind of paradise. Jesus saw his death as 'a ransom for many', the payment for the salvation of a multitude of others. This is actually the very purpose of his mission, the reason why he has been sent by God his Father.

How was this salvation to be accomplished, and how would Jesus' death be brought about? The second of the three excerpts above has a phrase which is loaded with meaning: 'the Son of Man *is to be handed over*'. There is calculated ambiguity here. In the first place, God has sent Jesus into the world to fulfil this task of atonement for sins through death. So God—on one level— presides over the whole process, such that it can be said that 'the Son of Man is to be handed over' *by God*. But the divine plan comes to its fulfilment in the earthly sphere through various human forces and causes. In the end, the Romans carry out the execution. Previously, the chief priests and the elders had 'handed over' Jesus to Pontius Pilate (Mark 15: 1). Before that, however, Jesus is 'handed over' to the priests by Judas Iscariot. The very same action is said to have been *both* a scheme of Judas and the Jewish leaders *and* part of the divine plan. In sum, Judas in Mark's Gospel is characterized as a fully fledged member of the twelve disciples of Jesus, unconsciously playing his part in God's mysterious will even as he apparently takes the initiative in offering his services in the plot against his master.

Matthew's Gospel

Rather than focus on the frenetic activity of Jesus' ministry as Mark does, Matthew's Gospel takes more time to describe at length the substance of Jesus' *teaching*: the Sermon on the

Mount is one of five examples of this in Matthew. Still, Matthew was heavily reliant on Mark's Gospel as one of his sources, and this is clear in the way that a lot of the material mentioned above resurfaces in an almost identical form:

Judas, one of the twelve, came. With him was a crowd armed with swords and clubs, sent from the chief priests, *the scribes* and the elders. Now the 'betrayer' had agreed a sign with them: 'The one I kiss is the man; arrest him *and take him away securely.*' And *coming* immediately he approached *him* and said, 'Rabbi!' And he kissed him. (Mark 14: 43–5)	Judas, one of the twelve, came. With him was a *great* crowd armed with swords and clubs, sent from the chief priests and the elders *of the people*. Now the 'betrayer' had agreed a sign with them: 'The one I kiss is the man; arrest him.' And immediately he approached *Jesus* and said, '*Greetings*, Rabbi!' And he kissed him. (Matt. 26: 47–9)

However, Matthew clearly has sources which supply additional information as well. First of all, Matthew includes a snippet of conversation between Jesus and Judas which is not paralleled in Mark:

Jesus answered, 'He who has dipped his hand in the dish with me is the one who will betray me. The Son of Man will go as it is written of him, but woe to that man through whom the Son of Man is betrayed! It would have been better for him if he had not been born.' *Judas, who was to betray him, answered, 'Is it I, Rabbi?' Jesus said to him, 'You have said so.'* (Matt. 26: 23–5)

This last piece of dialogue reveals an important fact about the relationship between Jesus and Judas: that according to the New Testament Jesus knew not only *that* he was going to be betrayed and executed, but also *who* his betrayer would be. As we will see, this is an important ingredient in the *Gospel of Judas*: there Jesus utters a prophecy to Judas about the latter's infamous deed, and perhaps even (though this is less certain) thereby instructs him to carry it out.

Jesus' knowledge about the betrayal comes to particularly poignant expression later in Matthew's Gospel:

Now the 'betrayer' had agreed a sign with them: 'The one I kiss is the man; seize him.' And he immediately approached *Jesus* and said, '*Greetings*, Rabbi!' And he kissed him. *Jesus said to him, 'Friend, do what you came to do.'* Then they came up and took Jesus and arrested him. (Matt. 26: 48–50)

It is this last statement by Jesus which is tantalizing. Again, it shows that Jesus knew who his betrayer was going to be. But does it go a stage further and imply that there is some sort of understanding between the two?

No—in fact, Matthew does not go this far. For one thing, the Greek of Jesus' statement here is rather ambiguous: translators disagree over whether it is a question ('Friend, why have you come?') or a command ('Friend, do what you have come for!') One commentary actually lists nine possible translations that have been suggested by scholars![3] If it is a command, however, it is much more likely that Jesus is shaming Judas by implying his knowledge of what is about to happen, rather than that he is giving his blessing to what Judas is about to do.

This much is obvious from the way in which Jesus had already made his views about the betrayer and his actions quite clear, as we saw in the quotation above from Matthew 26: 23–5: 'The Son of Man will go as it is written of him, but woe to that man through whom the Son of Man is betrayed! It would have been better for him if he had not been born' (v. 24). This of course makes it very difficult to see a special understanding between Jesus and Judas in the Gospel of Matthew.

Moving to a later stage in Matthew's account, one of the perennially controversial passages has been the account of Judas's remorse and suicide:

Then when Judas, who betrayed him, saw that Jesus was condemned, he changed his mind and brought back the thirty pieces of silver to the chief priests and the elders, saying, 'I have sinned by handing over/betraying innocent blood.' They said, 'What has that to do with us? That is your concern.' And throwing down the pieces of silver into the temple, he departed, and he went away and hanged himself. (Matt. 27: 3–5)

Matthew, then, supplements Mark's account with an extra layer of complexity to the role and character of Judas. This is no simple vilification on Matthew's part; rather there is an interweaving of two motifs in tension with one another. On the one hand, Matthew includes the account of Judas's death by hanging, which would have evoked something of a shudder from those listening to the Gospel being read out (there would have been relatively few *readers* in the earliest churches). This reaction would not have come primarily because of suicide being taboo—there was disagreement among Jews about that. It was more the *method*: for any Jew, 'a hanged man is an object accursed of God' (Deut. 21: 23). So Judas's suicide apparently intends not only to bring an end to his misery, but actually to bring on himself the divine punishment which he feels he deserves.

But if Matthew includes this self-inflicted curse, he also includes Judas's *remorse*: Judas at least, in contrast to Pontius Pilate, the priests, and others, regrets his actions. So Matthew's portrayal is a complex one, and is unique in constructing a portrait of Judas which perhaps in part aims to elicit some measure of pity for him. This is of course not the overriding emphasis, which is to follow along much the same lines as Mark.

Luke's Gospel

Luke's Gospel is the longest of the four New Testament Gospels and is unique among them in being the first instalment of a two-volume work. The Gospel and its sequel, the *Acts of the Apostles*, together make up approximately one-quarter of the New Testament, making Luke the single largest contributor to the collection.

The account of Jesus' life, death, and resurrection in this book has some important distinguishing features. In literary terms, Luke incorporates a large collection of parables which are not recorded in the other Gospels (the 'Good Samaritan' and the 'Prodigal Son', for example). Theologically, Luke is particularly interested in the spiritual forces (particularly evil forces) influencing the characters all through his account, and emphasizes this more than any of the other evangelists. We can see this, by way of a bean-counting aside, from how frequently 'Satan', 'the Devil', 'Beelzebul', 'demons', and unclean/evil 'spir-its' are mentioned by the four evangelists (see Table 2.1). This concern on Luke's part helps to explain why his account of the betrayal begins with the chilling words: 'Satan entered Judas . . . ' (Luke 22: 3). The bare events are much the same as we have seen in Mark and Matthew: Jesus knows he is being betrayed and that it is all taking place as divinely ordained; Judas comes to Jesus after the meal with soldiers and identifies him with a kiss. But Judas's actions are seen in a more sinister light because of Luke's narration not only of the human interactions but also of

Table 2.1. References to spiritual forces in the Gospels

	Matthew	Mark	Luke	John
Satan	3	5	6	1
the Devil	6	—	6	3
Beelzebul	3	1	3	—
demons	11	13	22	6
spirits	4	14	12	—

the supernatural forces underlying them. Interwoven into the account of the betrayal is another example of this tendency on Luke's part: he describes Jesus telling Simon Peter that Satan is also—this time unsuccessfully—trying to get hold of Peter (Luke 22: 31–2). There is an unseen world of forces at work in the events surrounding Jesus' arrest and execution that is highlighted in this Gospel more than in Matthew and Mark, and so Judas is painted by Luke as collaborating with those forces, just as he is in league with the chief priests in the events on earth.

John's Gospel

Since antiquity, John's Gospel has been recognized as a somewhat different kettle of fish from the other three Gospels. In around 190 CE, Clement of Alexandria described it as a 'spiritual Gospel',[4] and in one of its most striking statements Jesus, quite literally, demonizes Judas: 'Jesus replied to them, "Have I not chosen you, the twelve? And yet one of you is a devil." He spoke of Judas the son of Simon Iscariot, for he, one of the twelve, was going to betray him' (John 6: 70–1). This passage, probably the most negative statement about Judas in the four New Testament Gospels, has obviously contributed a great deal to the reputation of Judas down the centuries. Yet it should also be remembered that Jesus said much the same to—of all people—Simon Peter in the Gospels of Matthew and Mark. When Peter refused to accept what Jesus said about the necessity of the crucifixion, Jesus replied, 'Get behind me, Satan' (Mark 8: 33/Matt. 16: 23). So the accusation of being a devil is not *so* rare that it could only be attributed to someone like Judas, which is not to say that it is mere literary flourish either. John does, like Luke, attribute Judas's action to diabolical inspiration: 'During supper, the devil had already put it into the heart of Judas Iscariot, Simon's son, to betray him ... ' (John 13: 2). It is at this supper that John describes Jesus telling Judas, 'What you have to do, do quickly.' This statement we will come to later in the chapter.

One new feature of John's characterization of Judas is that he is mentioned as being the disciples' treasurer, and that he was a thief who often had his hands in the till: 'having charge of the moneybag, he used to take from what was put into it' (John 12: 6). But much of the material about the actual betrayal in John overlaps with the accounts in Matthew, Mark, and Luke: Jesus predicts his betrayal at the supper, and then Judas meets Jesus again later with the troops who are going to carry out the arrest. In fact, although this 'spiritual Gospel' often retells events in the ministry of Jesus from a perspective different from that of the other Gospels, and records a number of incidents not in Matthew, Mark and Luke, the common ground in the descriptions of Judas is considerable. There is the significance attached in all four Gospels (in slightly different ways) to dipping bread into the dish (Mark 14: 20/Matt. 26: 23 and John 13: 26). John has in common with Luke the reference to Satan inspiring Judas to his betrayal. John perhaps shares with Matthew the description of Jesus urging Judas on to carry out his miserable deed (John 13: 37 and Matt. 26: 50). In all four Gospels, Judas arrives with an armed band of soldiers. So the fourth Gospel is not so 'spiritual' that it has lost touch with historical reality.

The Acts of the Apostles

The account in Acts differs from the previous four versions we have looked at thus far. This work covers not the life of Jesus, but the earliest years of the Church, and as we have said is written by the author of Luke's Gospel as a sequel to it. As such, Acts does not narrate the betrayal of Jesus, but rather begins by relating his ascension and the return of the disciples to Jerusalem thereafter. The next event is a speech by Peter in which he announces that Judas's desertion was a fulfilment of Scripture; Judas acquired a field with the money he received; he died a gruesome death, and a new apostle must be selected to take his place (Acts 1: 16–20).

It is the manner of Judas's death that has perplexed scholars most here. As we have seen, Matthew apparently reports that Judas 'hanged himself' (Matt. 27: 5); on the other hand, in Acts, Peter comments that he 'fell headlong' or 'swelled up', and burst open with his bowels spewing forth (Acts 1: 18). A number of scholars have concluded that the two versions are incompatible, but, equally, many theologians in the history of the Church have explained them as complementary. St Augustine, for example,

argued that Judas did hang himself, but the rope broke and
he fell headlong and then died. A number of problems beset
both the critical and the harmonizing approaches. First, the
accounts in Matthew and Acts only add up to a very small
amount of information, and so part of the difficulty is that we
simply do not really have enough facts for an accurate historical reconstruction. Second, there is considerable ambiguity, as
scholars constantly note, in the account in Acts: it is extremely
hard to decide whether 'falling headlong' or 'swelling up' is the
translation to be preferred. The ambiguity here means that two
very different pictures can arise even from this single report in
Acts.

The focus of Luke's account here is not on the coroner's
report, however, but on the predetermined nature of the events
and Judas's terrible apostasy:

Brothers, the Scripture which the Holy Spirit spoke in advance by the
mouth of David concerning Judas, who became a guide to those who
arrested Jesus, had to be fulfilled. For he was numbered among us and
was allotted his share in this ministry. But he acquired a field with the
reward of his wickedness, and falling headlong [or, 'swelling up'] his
stomach burst open and all his bowels gushed out ... And they prayed
and said, 'You, Lord, who know the hearts of all, show which one
of these two you have chosen to take the place in this ministry and
apostleship from which Judas turned aside to go to his own place.'
(Acts 1: 16–18, 24–5)

Peter stresses, then, the fact that Judas shared in all the privi-
leges of the ministry of the disciples. Going back to the Gospel
narratives, this recalls the disciples' experiences of casting out
demons and healing, as well of witnessing the continual activity of Jesus. In rejecting all this, Peter implies, Judas was well

deserving of a shameful fate, however we are to picture the details. As we will see, the *Gospel of Judas* regards Judas's withdrawal from the apostolic circle as having been commanded by Jesus, but Acts sees Judas as having taken the law into his own hands and having thereby fallen into apostasy.

NEW TESTAMENT QUESTIONS

Having looked at the individual contributions of the New Testament authors, a number of questions emerge, especially given the pictures of Judas which have been developed over the centuries. Although there are some questions which are ultimately unanswerable, such as why exactly Judas chose to betray Jesus, some of the most important issues can be tackled.

Is Judas's Role Historical?

One of the most provocative challenges to the traditional understanding of Judas's role is to discount it altogether. In 1992, Hyam Maccoby argued that the early Christian community invented what we know as the conventional character of Judas. After an interesting opening chapter on 'Judas in the Western Imagination', Maccoby notes that the apostle Paul in the 50s CE talks about the risen Jesus appearing to 'the Twelve' (1 Cor. 15: 5), but the Gospel writers (from the 60s onwards) refer consistently to the *eleven*:

Our conclusion must be, therefore, that no tradition of the betrayal and defection of Judas existed before 60 CE. Before this date, Judas was regarded as a faithful apostle who mourned the death of Jesus together with the others and shared their experience of his resurrection. The whole story of the betrayal was invented not less than thirty years after Jesus's death...[5]

It is not surprising that very few scholars have followed Maccoby on this, however. He constructs his case simply on the basis of this hasty argumentation, and it is quite surprising to find the phrase 'our conclusion must be...' only three or four pages into the main body of the book. As the majority of scholars note, when Paul talks about Jesus appearing to 'the Twelve', he uses the phrase not for mere numerical reasons, but in the sense of 'a formal title for the corporate apostolic witness of those who had also followed Jesus during his earthly life, and who therefore underlined the continuity of witness to the One who was both crucified and raised.'[6] Jewish literature around the time of Paul was full of reference to official bodies of twelve members. Philo and Josephus talk of the twelve Old Testament princes of the Israelite tribes, and the Dead Sea Scrolls refer variously to an official 'twelve' in a court and in a council.[7] Hence, Paul could refer to the disciples as 'the Twelve' with more of a focus on them as an 'apostolic college' than as a particular number. So the main plank in Maccoby's argument for the invention of Judas's role is—as the majority of scholars have noted—decidedly shaky.

Do the Gospel Writers Distort Judas's Original Intention?

One scholar involved in the National Geographic's *Gospel of Judas* documentary, William Klassen, accepts that Judas plays a role in Jesus' death, but attempts to rehabilitate Judas on other grounds. He argues—on this point, correctly—that the word translated as 'betray' in English Bibles in fact generally means 'hand over'. Judas, Klassen goes on, was not a betrayer but an *informer*, and he hands Jesus over not out of greed or malice, but out of a sincere desire to facilitate a summit meeting between Jesus and the High Priest, perhaps so that they could sort out their differences.

Klassen submits his hypothesis as 'at least as plausible as the very negative view of Judas that still pervades the church'.[8] But in fact there is no real substance to it. Klassen mentions that as far as Judas was concerned, 'the last idea that would have entered his head was that his action might lead to Pilate's court and Jesus' death'.[9] This may rehabilitate Judas's good intentions, but it instead makes him out to be extremely stupid, given that according to the Gospels the Pharisees and others had been planning for some time to have Jesus executed (e.g. Mark 3: 6). Furthermore, what are we to make of Judas's arrival with 'a crowd armed with swords and clubs, sent from the chief priests, the scribes and the elders' (Mark 14: 43)? Klassen conveniently skates over this scene very quickly. He does give an explanation, however, for why Judas was offered money by the priests: it merely made the contract binding and valid 'as was the custom in such cases'.[10] This is nothing but speculation, however. Finally, the fact that all the other disciples are mortified at the suggestion that they might hand Jesus over suggests that for them it is a reprehensible act: 'And while they were reclining and eating, Jesus said, "Truly, I say to you, one of you who is eating with me will hand me over." They became sorrowful and said to him one after another, "Is it I?" ' (Mark 14: 18–19). This in fact confirms the conventional view that Judas's action cannot be explained as one which Jesus would have been in sympathy with; it can only be interpreted as having a sinister purpose, and in this respect the Gospels are all in agreement.

One passage which has not been sufficiently exploited in this debate is Judas's lament in Matthew 27: 4: 'I have sinned by handing over/betraying *innocent* blood.' The implication of Judas's statement is that it may well have been right and proper to 'hand over' a guilty person, but that Judas's action was sinful because Jesus had committed no crime. The Greek word *paradidōmi* ('hand over') is in itself neutral, but it is faulty logic to conclude from this that Judas's *act* is therefore neutral. The word (at least in the Gospel narratives here) refers to the two elements of *informing on*, and of physically *delivering* the accused—the assumption being that the informer knows the accused to have committed a crime. So Judas's action would have been quite legitimate had the accused been guilty, but takes on an utterly dark character when it is Jesus—the innocent man *par excellence*—who is the one turned in. Because Judas is also doing this to his master and friend (see especially Matt. 26: 50), the action can probably be seen as a betrayal as well.

Is Judas the Stereotype of the Evil Jew?

Christian history is full of a great deal of behaviour which is decidedly *un*christian, and the anti-Jewish character of some of the Church's theology and behaviour is a particularly regrettable part of that. Historians have also observed that the portrait of Judas has in some measure fuelled this (and, presumably, vice versa), largely on the basis of the connection (via 'Judaea') between his name and the word 'Jew'. Karl Barth is a twentieth-century example of this tendency to see Judas as embodying the nation of Israel:

Who is this Judas, the man who will maintain his freedom in face of Jesus for the sake of something better, the man for whom Jesus is for sale, who can also deliver Him up and surrender Him, and who has already done so in principle? Obviously he does not bear this name for nothing. Within the apostolic group—and this shows us what is meant by the uncleanness of the feet of all the apostles—he obviously represents the Jews, the stock from which both David himself and his promised Son sprang.[11]

But all this is really baseless. The New Testament never plays on the fact that Judas's *name* is somehow loaded with significance, or that he somehow embodies the world's or Judaism's opposition to Jesus. As far as the New Testament is concerned all the disciples, and of course Jesus himself, are just as Jewish as Judas.

Do the Gospel Writers Progressively Blacken Judas's Character?

Some scholars have inferred from the writings of the New Testament that there is an increasing tendency to demonize Judas as one Gospel follows another. Klassen has argued, for example, that with Judas 'there is a progressively degenerating trend in which he is portrayed in increasingly more negative terms.'[12]

The individual Gospel writers certainly had their own particular concerns and emphases. Matthew and Luke both expand the earliest account of Judas's role in the Gospel of Mark. But is Judas's character developed more negatively by Matthew than Mark? In fact, the principal addition by Matthew—the account of Judas's death—shows this hypothesis to be rather simplistic. This extra narrative makes the point that Judas is a cursed figure (as is implied by the hanging), but also mentions Judas's remorse. So Matthew's supplements to Mark are rather ambiguous as far as Judas is concerned.

Luke's account of the betrayal differs from those of his predecessors in that he states explicitly that Judas's activity in handing over Jesus was not merely a human decision, but one precipitated by evil, supernatural forces. But this is not because Luke suddenly pulls out all the stops to demonize Judas. We saw from the table above in our discussion of Luke that of all the evangelists Luke is most interested in the role of evil forces in the world generally, not just in the case of Judas. There are of course lies, damned lies, and statistics, but it protests too much to accuse Luke of a specifically 'anti-Judas' tendency on the basis of his statement that 'Satan entered Judas'.

By comparison with the other Gospels, John is distinctive in many ways, and so the different presentation of Judas there may not be necessarily because the author has particularly got it in for him. John probably does have the most negative portrayal of Judas in the New Testament, but even calling Judas a (or *the*) 'devil' is not to be taken literally: as we noted above, Jesus says to Simon Peter, 'get behind me, Satan' in the Gospels of Matthew and Mark. The accusation has more to do with which side Judas is on than with him actually being the Devil incarnate. In short, while the latest picture may be the most negative, there is certainly not the linear development of Judas's characterization in the New Testament ('a progressively degenerating trend in which he is portrayed in increasingly more negative terms') that Klassen imagines.

Judas in the New Testament

Did Jesus Tell Judas to Do It?

One of the most startling features of the *Gospel of Judas* is the revelation that in it Jesus announces to Judas, 'You will sacrifice the man who carries me about' (codex, p. 56). Even if Jesus is not explicitly instructing Judas to hand him over, he does appear to approve of what is to happen: the event goes hand in hand with Judas occupying his position as the 'leading star' (codex, p. 57). This has been taken to be one of the biggest differences between the *Gospel of Judas* and the four New Testament Gospels: in the canonical Gospels, Judas is working *against* Jesus, not in harmony with him.

But what of the mysterious statements in Matthew and John?

Jesus said to him, 'Friend, do what you came to do.' [*Or:* 'Friend, why are you here?'] Then they came up and took Jesus and arrested him. (Matt. 26: 50)

After Judas had taken the morsel, Satan entered into him. Jesus said to him, 'What you are going to do, do quickly.' None of those at the table knew why he said this to him. (John 13: 27–8)

There are difficulties with interpreting Matthew's statement here. As we have seen, in addition to the possibility of taking Jesus' words as a command, they can also be understood as a question or a statement instead. John's account, on the other hand, is perfectly clear: it can only be an instruction.

However, John's Gospel is not open to being read as approving of Judas's action here. What we have instead in the fourth Gospel is a continued emphasis not only that—as in Matthew, Mark, and Luke—Jesus knows he will be betrayed, but also that he knows exactly *when* it will happen. So in his early ministry,

Jesus makes some decisions on the basis of the fact that God's plan is not ready to be fulfilled:

'You go up to the feast. I am not going up to this feast, for my time is not yet fulfilled.' (John 7: 8)

This plan is specifically about the 'time' for Jesus' arrest:

So they tried to catch him, but no one laid a hand on him, because his hour had not yet come. (John 7: 30)

He spoke these words in the treasury, while he was teaching in the temple. But no one could catch him, because his hour had not yet come. (John 8: 20)

Eventually, of course, the time is ripe:

And Jesus answered them, 'The hour has come for the Son of Man to be glorified.' (John 12: 23)

Before the Feast of the Passover, Jesus knew that his hour had come to pass from this world to the Father. Having loved his own who were in the world, he loved them to the end. (John 13: 1)

It is soon after Jesus has made these last two statements that he tells Judas, 'What you are going to do, do quickly' (John 13: 27). The time has come. Satan has entered Judas. Jesus is ready to depart from the world.

CONCLUSION

To sum up the canonical portraits in the New Testament, we have Judas portrayed as very much an integral member of the twelve disciples, but as one who then, despite everything, becomes apparently inexplicably involved in the Passover plot.

At least, inexplicably on the human plane—there are dark forces at work which have inspired Judas to do his deed, while he is at the same time fully responsible for the initiative he takes in approaching the plotters. And yet this evil, both supernatural and human, is not actually the ultimate factor: Judas is playing his part in the *divine* drama, predicted in the Old Testament scriptures, which ultimately leads to Jesus' death for the salvation of his people. Judas—despite his remorse—comes to his end under the divine curse as he hangs on the tree, but Jesus' death (also under a curse on a tree, or wooden cross) brings God's plan for redemption to fruition, and is followed by resurrection.

We will see that the picture in the *Gospel of Judas* is rather different. But we do have already in the New Testament Jesus' command to Judas, 'What you are going to do, do quickly', even if—as we saw—this certainly does not imply that Jesus is giving his blessing to what Judas is about to do. Jesus knows what Judas is intending, and so tells him to get on with it since the occasion for it in God's purpose has now come. Yet it is possible to imagine how, extracted from the context in John's Gospel which has this great concern with the timing of God's purpose, those words could encourage the idea of Jesus' approval of the action. So the New Testament does perhaps contain some of the raw materials which, when juggled around, could prove congenial to our Gnostic author: not only the two main characters, but also some of Jesus' portentous words to Judas.

3

The Next 100 Years

A NUMBER of fascinating studies of Judas have already examined the way in which he has been portrayed through history,
whether as a representative of medieval Jewry, or as a redhead,
or as one suffering torments in Dante's *Inferno*. These later
developments lie outside the bounds of what is relevant for
our exploration of the *Gospel of Judas*. But what is particularly
germane here is the picture of Judas which developed in the
second century—the period, as we will argue in Chapter 6, in
which the *Gospel of Judas* was originally written. The person or
group behind the *Gospel of Judas* would have been aware not
only of the Judas of the New Testament but also of the popular
portrayals of Judas current in the author's own day. But in addition to seeing what the *Gospel of Judas* is reacting against, we can
also see in this period evidence—thus far neglected—of Gnostic
speculation about Judas which may well have contributed to the
shocking new role he plays in our newly discovered manuscript.

THE APOSTOLIC FATHERS: JUDAS THE ARCHETYPAL TRAITOR

Moving beyond the period of the Gospels and Acts, then, we
come to the references to Judas in literature known as the

'Apostolic Fathers'. Now that the events of Judas's last days were generally well established for the early Christians the focus moves to Judas being an archetypal villain.

The *Martyrdom of Polycarp* (written *c*.170 CE) already makes reference to Judas as a prototype traitor: those who betray the 86-year-old Polycarp, Bishop of Smyrna, are said to be destined for the same punishment as Judas. Other Christian works of the time (such as the *Shepherd of Hermas*) refer to traitors within the Church, as from the other side does the Roman opponent of the Christians, the younger Pliny.[1] Pliny, pleasant chap that he was, writes to the emperor in the early second century (*c*.111–112 CE), commenting that he has tried to get information about local Christians by torturing two female slaves, but that he also had an informer who denounced Christians to him. Additionally, it appears that Pliny made use of a list of alleged Christians which had been anonymously published. The emperor Trajan replies that such anonymous lists should not be used in Pliny's investigations, though Pliny has been right to use informers. This kind of talk provides an interesting backdrop against which to understand the reference in *Martyrdom of Polycarp*:

And since those who were searching for him [Polycarp] continued, he moved to another farm. And immediately those who were searching for him arrived, and because they did not find him, they seized two slave boys, one of whom confessed under torture. For it was impossible for him to hide, since those who betrayed him were members of his own household. And the police chief, who had the same name as Herod, as he was also called, hurried to bring him into the stadium, so that Polycarp might fulfil his appointed lot of being a sharer in Christ. But those who betrayed him received the punishment of Judas. (*Martyrdom of Polycarp*, 6)

Those who are pursuing Polycarp, then, follow the same policy as Pliny in order to find their man. Polycarp is given away by a tortured slave, and so becomes a martyr like Christ, as a result of which he will go with Christ after his death. But, just as Jesus establishes the pattern for his disciples to follow, so does Judas: those who betray the Church are following in his footsteps, and so his destiny awaits them as well.

The *Fragments of Papias* (*c*.130–140 CE) furnish some more examples of the picture of Judas in the second century CE. Papias was a Christian leader in Asia Minor in the early second century, and a friend of Polycarp. One of the fragments of his writing which has survived simply refers to Judas in a stereotyped way as 'the betrayer' or 'the traitor' (*Fragments* 3: 10). However, Judas is not only 'the betrayer' but also 'the unbeliever', in Papias's rather strange report of a forecast that the new world would consist of extraordinary prosperity:

The elders, who saw John the disciple of the Lord, remembered that they had heard from him how the Lord taught about those times and said: 'The days will come when vines will grow, each with ten thousand shoots, and on each shoot ten thousand branches, and on each branch ten thousand twigs, and on each twig ten thousand bunches, and on each bunch ten thousand grapes. And when each grape is pressed, it will yield twenty-five measures of wine . . . '

Papias, a hearer of John, a companion of Polycarp, and a man of the ancient time, bears witness to these things in his writing, in the fourth of his books (for there are five books composed by him). And he goes on to say: 'These things are believable to those who believe. But Judas,' he said, 'being an unbelieving traitor, asked, "How, then, will such growth be accomplished by the Lord?" The Lord said, "Those who come in those times will see." ' (*Fragment* 14, quoted in Irenaeus, *Against Heresies*, 5.33.3–4)

The oddity of the agricultural scene aside, it is noteworthy that here we have a picture not of Judas the secretive traitor, but of the one who openly doubts Jesus. This at least is Papias's spin on the alleged dialogue between Jesus and Judas: in fact, Judas's question here might be open to a rather more innocent interpretation. The dialogue is almost certainly legendary in any case, but there may be an attempt on Papias's part to paint Judas in an even more negative light than his source.

Finally, and most bizarrely of all, is Papias's last mention of Judas, passed on to us by the fourth-century writer Apollinaris. This Apollinaris seems to be attempting to understand both accounts of Judas's death (in the passages in Matthew and Acts discussed in Chapter 2) as being in agreement with one another, and in the course of his discussion brings in Papias's portrait of Judas:

Judas did not die by his hanging but lived on because he was cut down before he was strangled to death. The Acts of the Apostles shows this: 'swelling up, his stomach burst open and his intestines spilled out.' Papias, the disciple of John, recounts this more clearly in the fourth book of the *Exposition of the Sayings of the Lord*, as follows:

'Judas lived as an example of ungodliness in this world. His flesh was so swollen that where a wagon can easily pass he was not able to, not even his bloated head on its own. For the lids of his eyes, they say, were so swollen that he was not able to see light at all, and his eyes were impossible to see even for a doctor through an optical instrument, so deep had they gone below the outside of his face. His genitals were more disgusting and larger than those of anyone else, and when he relieved himself, pus and worms flowed through his whole body, to his shame. After great agonies and punishments, they say, he finally died in his own place: because of the smell, it is still deserted and uninhabitable; in fact, to this very day no one can pass that place unless they pinch their nose, because such a great amount of discharge passed from his body and onto the ground.' (Fragment 18, cited by Apollinaris)

This lends support to the suggestion that Papias may be out to paint Judas even more negatively than does the New Testament. This characterization of Judas as a swollen ogre ties in with an idea held by some in the ancient world that physical features were an indication of moral character—beauty signified a righteous person, ugliness the opposite. The Qumran community, for example, the Jewish group that gave us the Dead Sea Scrolls, apparently held to this kind of reasoning. One text talks about a two-column list of archetypal righteous and wicked people. In the first column are mentioned the characteristics of the wicked person and in the second the Law-observant, godly characters:

(first column)
His fingers are fat, and both his thighs are fat and hairy, each one. His toes are fat and short. His spirit has eight parts from the house of darkness and one from the house of light. (4Q186, Fragment 1, col. iii)

(second column)
And his thighs are long and slim, and his toes are slim and long. He is of the second column. His spirit has six parts from the house of light and three from the house of darkness. (ibid., col. ii)

With the description of Judas constructed along the same sorts of principles, we are clearly in the realms of early Christian legend here. It may well be that the author of the *Gospel of Judas* was familiar not only with the New Testament portrayals of Judas but also with some of the popular gossip which elaborated on them. In the Apostolic Fathers of the second century, Judas has become an unbeliever and paradigm of wickedness. He is not quite yet a cautionary tale ('don't be like Judas!'). But in the *Martyrdom of Polycarp* he is an archetypal traitor, the forerunner of those who denounced Christians in the persecutions of the second century, and in Papias, 'an example of ungodliness in this world'.[2]

EARLIEST APOCRYPHAL WRITINGS: JUDAS THE CAUTIONARY TALE

The literature from the Apostolic Fathers tends to be doctrinal and ethical for the most part. In contrast, the apocryphal (or, non-canonical) Gospels and Acts are more often narratives, and of an even more imaginative nature. They expand on what Jesus and his disciples might have said and done in incidents not reported in the comparable but earlier New Testament writings.

One point which is accentuated in this literature is the diabolical inspiration of Judas, as for example in the *Acts of Peter* (*c*.180 CE):

But when Peter saw this, he was shaken with grievous sorrow and said: 'What manifold tricks and temptations the devil has! What machinations and contrivances of the wicked! That ravening wolf, the devourer and waster of eternal life, is preparing for the day of wrath a great fire for himself, as well as the destruction of simple men! You caught the first man in the net of desire, and bound him with your ancient wickedness and the chain of the body. You are the most bitter fruit of that tree of bitterness, you who induce manifold desires. You caused Judas, my fellow disciple and apostle, to betray our Lord Jesus Christ who must now punish you. You hardened the heart of Herod, and inflamed Pharaoh . . . (*Acts of Peter*, 8)

Here Judas comes in a long list of biblical villains portrayed as having been stirred up to do their acts of wickedness by the Devil himself. As we have seen, this evil inspiration is already mentioned by Luke and John, and the tradition is embellished in the *Acts of Thomas*, which probably dates from a time slightly later than the *Acts of Peter*—from the early third century CE. This work also gives a list of villainous acts, this time in a speech put into the mouth of the serpent in the Garden of Eden, who is apparently the offspring of Satan:

'I am a reptile born of reptile nature, a woeful creature born of a woeful father...I am the one who entered through the fence in Paradise and said to Eve all the things which my father commanded me to say to her; I am the one who kindled and inflamed Cain to kill his own brother...I am he who inflamed Herod and kindled Caiaphas in his false accusation to Pilate. This is what I am like. I am the one who kindled Judas and bribed him so that he would betray Christ to death...' (*Acts of Thomas*, 32)

Judas actually comes at the end of this list, and the serpent that we know from the Garden of Eden is apparently the same figure that inspired both Judas and those who offered him the money.

Interestingly, the *Acts of Thomas* refers to Judas again, this time in even closer proximity to Cain:

so, first, keep away from adultery, for it is the beginning of all evils; and from murder, for which the curse came upon Cain; and then from theft, which ensnared Judas Iscariot and led him to his hanging; and from intemperance, for which Esau lost his birthright... (*Acts of Thomas*, 84)

Here, then, Judas becomes a negative example: one should obey the ten commandments, or else fall in with the company of Cain, Judas, and Esau, and so share in the punishments which they received for their disobedience. In this account, Judas's theft from the treasury in John's Gospel is linked with his betrayal of Jesus; they are part and parcel of the same thing— Judas's greedy thieving. His consequent hanging, although it would certainly still have been imagined as suicide, was at the same time regarded as God's punishment of Judas.

In this literature, then, the familiar theme of Judas's betrayal of course continues to crop up. But, as in the Apostolic Fathers, it is not only the decisive event of Judas's role in the execution of Jesus that is emphasized; in fact, Judas's actions are in danger of being repeated by others who might be entangled by greed and theft. In the *Acts of Thomas*, Judas becomes for the first time explicitly a negative role-model, someone held up as a counter-example whose behaviour is to be avoided. And he is an illustration of the fact that such entanglements come not only from human impulses, but as the results of darker forces at work.

THE GNOSTIC JUDAS

The last portrait of Judas to mention here is one which may be very relevant to the *Gospel of Judas*, but which has not been picked up in any of the literature on the new-found text so far. In the accounts of Judas mentioned already in this chapter, we have seen a mix of the human side of the story, in which Judas is the perpetrator of Jesus' betrayal, and the supernatural aspects of the case, in which demonic forces are involved. But a further level of complexity has emerged by around 180 CE in the time of St Irenaeus. This early Church leader (on whom more in Chapter 5) wrote a monumental attack on the Gnostics, the movements mentioned in the Introduction as characterized by belief in a separation of the supreme deity from the lesser creator God and the dozens of other divinities who populated the heavens. According to some of the Gnostics whom Irenaeus mentions, Judas was embroiled in the heavenly Gnostic drama of chaos and salvation, and was related to the divine 'aeons' (heavenly realms, or deities). So the *Gospel of Judas* is not the only work to have developed a Gnostic conception of Judas; he was integral to the development of some major themes in Gnostic mythology, and has a role of his own in some traditions.

Judas's Influence on the Sophia Myth

First, Judas appears to have had an influence on some versions of the myth of the goddess 'Sophia' (Greek for 'wisdom'), a deity who has a fall from grace which is central to a number of Gnostic systems. She is a psychoanalyst's delight, because in Gnostic tradition she can paradoxically represent both Madonna-like virginity and, as here, fallen womanhood. Some traditions maintain this paradox, while others attempt to resolve it by splitting Sophia into a 'higher Sophia' (a saviour) and a 'lower Sophia'—referred to on one occasion as 'the Sophia of death'.[3]

One cause of Sophia's fall is that she has ideas above her station and acts without the permission of her consort: she has a male partner whom naively she does not consult in her desire to see the supreme power or (as in other versions of the myth) in her generation of offspring.[4] The result of this is that she is nearly separated permanently from the 'pleroma', the fullness of the divine realm (and in versions of the story in which she gives birth, she generates defective offspring). But Sophia's fall is not final. She is restored—and is described in one tradition at least as being redeemed by Christ coming to her.

Two brief passages from Irenaeus will illustrate versions of the Sophia myth:

But there rushed forth, in advance of the rest, the Aeon who was the last and youngest of the Duodecad (i.e., the 'twelve'), namely Sophia. She had been emitted from Anthropos and Ecclesia. And she suffered a passion apart from the embrace of her consort Theletos. (*Against Heresies*, 1.2.2)

And for this reason, since a fall had taken place around the twelfth number, the sheep gambolled off, and went astray—because, they say, a defection [*or*, apostasy] took place from the Duodecad. In the same way they also oracularly declare that the one power which seceded from the Duodecad was lost, and that this is seen in the woman who lost the drachma, lit her her lamp, and again found it. (ibid., 1.16.1)

Despite the reference to the parable of the lost coin (Luke 15: 8–10), Judas is more likely to have been the dominant influence here. (The woman had ten coins, not twelve.) Judas's influence on the Sophia myth can be seen from the fact that Sophia, like him, is one of a 'twelve', the last of this twelve, and who defects from the group.

The connection between Sophia and Judas at this point is made explicit by a comment of Epiphanius (writing in the 370s CE) who talks of Judas and the aeon in question both being 'the twelfth', and both defecting:

Moreover they say that the twelfth aeon, which became defective, dropped out from the number of the twelve completely, and the twelfth number was lost. They say that this is what happened in the defection of Judas, the twelfth, and that this is how the twelfth number disappeared. (*Panarion*, 31.35, 2–3; see also 31.14, 9)

Epiphanius here is really only drawing on material present already in Irenaeus, as we can see from Irenaeus's other treatments of the theme.

Judas the Image of the Twelfth Aeon

One of Irenaeus's central concerns in his work is to counter what he sees as the excessively imaginative speculations in the Gnostics' interpretations of the Bible. One case in point is the idea that Judas is identified as an 'image', or 'type', or 'emblem' of the twelfth aeon (the twelfth locale or zone in the heavens). This Gnostic theme of entities in the earthly world being images of heavenly realities is a regular target for Irenaeus. He attacks the principle in general, then the idea as it is applied by some of his Gnostic opponents to the twelve disciples, and finally the particular case of Judas:

So we will demonstrate that they apply both the parables and the actions of the Lord improperly and inconsistently in their false scheme. For one, they try to demonstrate that the passion took place in connection with the twelfth aeon, from the fact that the passion of the Saviour was brought about by the twelfth apostle in the twelfth month. For they wishfully think that he preached for only one year after his baptism. (*Against Heresies*, II.20, 1; cf. I.3, 3)

Irenaeus then paraphrases them further as saying that Judas is a 'type' of this aeon, because 'she is indicated in Judas', and he is 'the type and image of that aeon who suffered' (20, 2).[5]

The Next 100 Years

Judas Identified with the Twelfth Aeon

Thirdly, if the reports in the Church Fathers are accurate, Judas can also himself be called an aeon. This idea is found in a tradition about the second-century Marcus Magus, recorded by the heresiologist Philastrius (writing around 383–391 CE):

He [Marcus] also said that, in the last time, the Christ descended on Jesus in the form and likeness of a dove, and taught that Christ was himself the dove which, he said, 'descended to the twelve aeons', that is, to the twelve apostles. And he considered that one of them had fallen, that is, Judas. (*Book of Diverse Heresies*, 42, 3)

This is striking because in Philastrius here the language of Judas as 'image' or 'emblem' has disappeared: the disciples are simply identified with the twelve aeons, and Judas logically as both twelfth apostle and twelfth aeon. This is confirmed by the final sentence, in which Marcus 'considered that one of them had fallen, that is, Judas'. This would make no sense as an observation merely of the historical Judas's apostasy and fate; it would be completely redundant to identify this as a distinctive point which Marcus 'considered', because it was the standard view. Marcus's idea here is almost certainly that it is the 'Judas-aeon', the twelfth aeon, which fell: in other words, Judas is coming very close actually to being identified with Sophia.

A New Judas?

Finally, to indulge in speculation, it is perhaps imaginable how after Judas had exercised a strong influence on the Sophia myth, the two figures became so closely intertwined that the influence then began to work in the other direction as well. One possible instance of this is Sophia 'grieving deeply' (*Against Heresies*, 1.29.4)—a theme which finds a parallel in the *Gospel of Judas*, where Judas will 'grieve greatly' (codex, p. 35; cf. p. 57).

Furthermore, it may also be that not only are the negative elements of Sophia's and Judas's characters in the picture, but that some of Sophia's *positive* characteristics have rubbed off on Judas as well. We will see in the *Gospel of Judas* that the character of Judas there—like Sophia in some Gnostic systems— is regarded as holy, and given a position of cosmic supremacy. He is depicted as a kind of ideal priest who will make a great sacrifice and after a period of suffering be elevated to glory. He is to drop out of the twelve, on Jesus' instructions, and the twelve will be restored by the addition of another (codex, pp. 35–6). As a result, Judas is the 'thirteenth spirit' (p. 44) and will be the star which rules over both the other disciples (pp. 46, 56–7) and the thirteenth aeon (p. 55). Although there is no smoking-gun proof here, it may be that these Gnostic ideas about Sophia as reported by Irenaeus and others played a role in the construction of this new Judas.

CONCLUSION

So, as we mentioned at the outset, there are at least two ways in which the material in this chapter fleshes out the background to the *Gospel of Judas*. In the first place, we have the development of the traditional picture. Taking the Gospels and Acts as its point of departure, this literature from the second century portrays Judas as an ogre and a paradigmatic figure—in the *Martyrdom of Polycarp* a prototype traitor and in the *Acts of*

Thomas the most notorious example of thieving. So the developing portrait of Judas in this period is even more negative than is the New Testament. As background to the *Gospel of Judas*, this gives us a good impression of the kind of images of Judas against which this radically new picture is reacting.

On the other hand, we have also seen some of the possible raw materials which the author of the *Gospel of Judas* may have found more congenial to his task. The ideas discussed by Irenaeus, Epiphanius, and Philastrius link Judas with the twelfth Gnostic aeon, a position also occupied by 'Sophia'. Since Irenaeus is writing in the second century and Philastrius associates these ideas with the second-century Marcus, it is worth considering whether the author of our Judas text may have been drawing on these unconventional thoughts.

4

Translation and Interpretation

Key

bold type	translation of the text
<33>, <34>, etc.	manuscript page numbering
[text in square brackets]	conjecture for lost text
{text in pointed brackets}	probable scribal error
. . .	approximately one word illegible
. . . . . .	approximately half a line missing
(x lines missing)	larger amount of lost text

Prologue

<33> **The secret message of the revelation which Jesus spoke to Judas Iscariot in the week leading up to the third day before he celebrated Passover.**

The *Gospel of Judas* is a good example of a book signalling at the outset what kind of work it is. Like many 'Gnostic' writings, it claims to be secret revelation delivered to one person alone, hence Jesus' instructions later on that Judas should separate himself from the other disciples in order to hear

61

it (codex, p. 35). In this respect, the *Gospel of Judas* begins rather differently from the four New Testament Gospels, all of which focus on narrating the *public* ministry of Jesus: Luke 1: 1, for example, talks about 'the events which have been fulfilled among us'. According to the New Testament, Jesus did teach in private as well, but usually in the company of his twelve disciples, rather than disclosing secret revelation to single individuals. The prologue of the *Gospel of Judas* here aims at something similar to the introductory statements of works such as the *Gospel of Thomas*, or the *Book of Thomas the Contender*:

These are the secret sayings which the living Jesus spoke and which Didymus Judas Thomas wrote down. (*Gospel of Thomas*, prologue)[1]

The secret words which the Saviour spoke to Judas Thomas and which I, Mathaias, wrote down as I was walking, listening to them speak with one another. (*Thomas the Contender*, prologue)[2]

One Gnosticism scholar has classified these sorts of works as 'Gnostic revelation dialogues', which usually describe conversations, often in a question-and-answer format, between a favoured disciple or group of disciples and Jesus after his resurrection.[3] This fits the *Gospel of Judas* rather well: Judas, as we will see, is Jesus' chosen disciple and much of the revelation comes to him in answer to his questions. The difference in the case of the *Gospel of Judas* is obviously the time-frame: the revelation does not take place in the period between Jesus' resurrection and ascension. But this is understandable (and may account for why the author specifies the date of the events): Judas is dead before the death, resurrection, and ascension of Jesus, and so a setting after the resurrection of Jesus would make things rather awkward to say the least.

By contrast, then, this secret revelation of Jesus to Judas has its setting in the run-up to the third day before Passover. This time-frame fits with the date Matthew and Mark give for the plot against Jesus being set in motion: 'It was two days before the Passover and the Feast of Unleavened Bread. The chief priests and the scribes were trying somehow to arrest him by trickery and kill him' (Mark 14: 1; cf. Matt. 26: 2). There might seem to be a discrepancy of a day between these two versions, but in fact in the Roman calendar 'two days before' would have been expressed as 'the third day before.' (To take a famous example, the Ides of March fell on 15 March but the Romans would have written 13 March as 'ante diem *III* Id. Mart.'.) Alternatively, the idea could be that the revelations took place over the course of a week which ended on the third day before Passover, and then the chief priests approached Judas the next day.

The main surprise here, however, is the recipient of the revelation: Judas Iscariot. We have seen from our survey of the second-century literature in Chapter 3 that the passage of time in early Christian history did little to improve Judas's reputation; in fact, the opposite was the case. Even the suggestions we have made in Chapters 2 and 3 about some of the raw materials which our author here might have used take nothing away from how unusual it is to have Judas in this position.

Jesus' Public Ministry

When he appeared upon the earth, he performed signs and great wonders for the salvation of humanity. Since some were

[walking] in the way of righteousness, and others were walking in their transgression, the twelve disciples were called. He began to speak to them the mysteries above the world, and the things to come to pass at the end. And a number of times he did not reveal himself to his disciples, but could be found as a child in their midst.

The pattern of the *Gospel of Judas* is to begin, here, with the widest sphere of Jesus' activity, before moving next to Jesus' interaction with the disciples, and finally to the tête-à-tête with Judas. Much of what is said in this brief account of Jesus' ministry could equally be a summary of the four Gospels in the New Testament, at least before the cross and resurrection. But the line of thought in this section is still not quite obvious. Even the first sentence is unclear—is 'the salvation of humanity' *achieved*? Or do the 'signs and wonders' actually not have the desired effect? The sentence following seems to imply that the purpose is not fulfilled because some are sinners, and so a special cohort of helpers is needed, to be instructed in supernatural mysteries and the events of the end.

The term 'appeared' at the beginning is a common one in the *Gospel of Judas*; here it refers to—or rather, as we will see, is an alternative to—the incarnation. The mysterious reference to Jesus revealing himself as a child is actually not so unusual in Gnostic and related writings. There are numerous examples, including the statement of Valentinus: 'And Valentinus said that he had seen a new-born infant child, and inquiring, he sought to know who he was. And he (the child) answered and said that he was the Logos.'[4]

The language used of the disciples here is also subtly suggestive: 'the twelve disciples were called'. But called by whom? The obvious answer to this question is *Jesus*, but the passage does not actually say so. And in fact, although they are called 'his' disciples on a number of occasions, the attitude which Jesus will later display to the disciples and the evil god to whom they belong might raise doubts, though this is far from clear.[5]

Part I: Polemic Against the 'Great Church'
The first part of the document is mainly a series of scenes in which Jesus attacks the twelve disciples (Judas sometimes excepted). The reason for this tirade is not merely an attempt to rehabilitate Judas in contrast to the others; rather the point lies in the assumption in the author's surrounding milieu that people regarded the wider, non-Gnostic Church as founded by and upon the twelve apostles—and so to criticize the twelve is to attack the whole mainstream Church.

Although there has been a good deal of opposition to the idea that there was such a 'mainstream' Church early on built on the foundation of the apostles, this was nevertheless the way both the non-Gnostic Christian Church saw itself, and how it was defined by dissident groups, such as the Gnostics. In fact, the relationship between the 'orthodox' church and smaller sectarian groups was also viewed in a similar light by at least some pagans: Celsus (writing perhaps between 177 and 180 CE) referred to the orthodox Christian establishment which he was attacking as 'the great church'.[6]

Launching similar attacks around the time of the *Gospel of Judas* were other 'alternative' Gospels from the second century CE. They too adopted their own patron apostles who, they maintained, had received secret revelation from Jesus which the other disciples had not. We noted the *Gospel of Thomas* above, and its prologue to this effect: this work also has Jesus casting aside the views that other key disciples (Simon and Matthew) had of him, in preference for the true revelation possessed by Thomas.[7]

This strategy in the *Gospel of Thomas* is very similar to the approach adopted by the *Gospel of Judas*. What survives from the first part of the work here consists of three days, the events of which combine to establish the foolishness and corruption of the apostolate of the twelve disciples. This first part thereby clears the ground by writing off any Church and theological system which is founded on these twelve disreputables. In the mean time, it begins to advance Judas as the figure who is going to be the special recipient of the revelation, although this is primarily the focus in Part II (which is rather longer than the first part), as we will see.

Day 1: Jesus Mocks the Disciples' Piety; Judas comes to the Fore
And one day in Judaea he came to the disciples and he found them sitting gathered practising their piety. When he [met] his disciples <34> sitting gathered and giving thanks over the bread, he laughed.

The disciples said to him, 'Master, why do you laugh at [our] thanksgiving? What have we done? This is what is right.'

He answered, and said to them, 'I am not laughing at you: you are not doing this by your own will, but because by it your god [receives] praise.'

They said, 'Master, you ... are the son of our god.'

Jesus said to them, 'How do you know me? Truly, [I] say to you, no generation among the men who are in your midst will know me.' But when his disciples heard this, they began to be annoyed and ... angry, and to blaspheme against him in their hearts.

This section begins with a very vague indication of date ('one day') and place (*Judaea* is an entire Roman province). Jesus *came to*, or came upon, the disciples in sudden mysterious appearance.[8] As we will see, Jesus appears and disappears repeatedly in the course of his dialogues.

The word for the 'thanksgiving' in which the disciples are involved here is *eucharistia*, which almost creates the impression that Jesus has walked in on a church service. In his *First Apology* (from around 150 CE), the early Christian writer Justin Martyr describes 'eucharist' as a technical term, referring to the food at the Christian 'communion' meal:

And this food is called among us the 'eucharist'. It is not permitted for anyone else to have a share in it except the one who believes that the things taught by us are true, who has been washed for the forgiveness of sins and rebirth, and who lives according to the way Christ has passed on to us. For we do not take this as common bread or common drink. Rather, just as Jesus Christ our Saviour, incarnate by the Word of God, had both flesh and blood for our salvation, so also we have been taught that the food which is blessed by the prayer of his word (from which our blood and flesh by transformation are also nourished) is the flesh and blood of the incarnate Jesus. For the apostles, in the memoirs written by them, which are called Gospels, have passed on to us what was enjoined upon them as follows. Jesus took bread, gave thanks, and said, 'Do this in remembrance of me: this is my body.' And similarly he took the cup, gave thanks and said, 'This is my blood.' And he gave it to them alone. (*First Apology*, Chapter 66)

This 'giving thanks over the bread', then, is probably considerably more than the disciples saying grace before the meal. As the National Geographic volume rightly notes, 'The specific language used here calls to mind ... the celebration of the eucharist within Christianity.'[9]

Jesus goes on to say that he is not mocking the disciples personally, but instead laughs at the god who demands this eucharist. At the same time, Jesus implies that he is not related to this god of the disciples: their description of Jesus ('the son of our god'), modelled on a statement of Simon Peter in the New Testament, is according to Jesus completely off the mark.[10] There is an absolute distinction between the ultimately supreme deity and the one worshipped by the disciples, as well as between those who really know Jesus, and the generation from which the disciples come. This theme of the 'generations', which appears for the first time here in the *Gospel of Judas*, will be an important recurring motif in the work.

Jesus' laughter comes as a surprise, further suggesting a rather different portrait of Jesus from that painted in the four canonical Gospels. The silence of the New Testament on this theme has been the subject of numerous historical debates within the Church—reflected expertly by Umberto Eco in *The Name of the Rose*. On a number of occasions the villain of this novel, the murderous Jorge of Burgos, spars with William of Baskerville on the subject. The former argues: 'Laughter is weakness, corruption, the foolishness of our flesh. It is the peasant's entertainment, the drunkard's license...'.[11] Jorge cites John Chrysostom that Jesus never laughed; the worldly Englishman William replies that nothing in Jesus' human nature would have prevented him from doing so. Maybe so, replies Jorge, but no record of Jesus' laughter is ever recorded in the Gospels.[12]

Medieval casuistry aside, there are some illuminating references in the Gnostic writings found near Nag Hammadi which have no hesitation in describing Jesus as laughing. In the *Apocalypse of Peter*, for example, there is a shocking scene in which the crucified earthly body of Jesus is being crucified, but with him the *living* Jesus stands by laughing at the stupidity of those around.[13] 'Laughing' in Gnostic literature is almost always a mockery of the stupidity of blind human beings or of the 'archons', wicked heavenly powers.

We will explore later how in some of the *Gospel of Judas* litera-ture that has already appeared, the laughter here has prompted some to conclude that Jesus in this work is a more down-to-earth and friendly figure than he is in the four New Testament Gospels (more on this in Chapter 7).[14] Suffice it to say here that Jesus' mirth in this scene is clearly scornful laughter, rather than avuncular amusement or hearty guffawing.

As we said in the introduction to this first part, the point here is the polemic against the wider Church which regarded the twelve disciples as the foundation of that Church. The *Gospel of Judas* is in the process of constructing a full-scale attack on these disciples by accusing them of being wrong about their core theological belief: they are ignorant of the identity of both Jesus and the deity who sent him.

But when Jesus saw their stupidity, [he said] to them, 'Why this angry agitation? Your god who is within you and ... <35> annoyed, with your souls. Let whoever is [strong] among you men bring forth the perfect man and stand in the presence of my face.'

And they all said, 'We are strong enough.' But their spirits were not bold enough to stand in his presence, except Judas Iscariot. While he was able to stand in his presence, he could not look into his eyes, but turned his face away.

Judas [said] to him, 'I know who you are and from where you have come. You have come from the immortal aeon of

Barbelo and the one who sent you is the one whose name I am not worthy to speak.'

The characterization of the disciples here is a paradoxical one: on the one hand they are ignorant, but they also have a spark of the divine within them. This is a common Gnostic theme, and a key point at which the Gnostic theological system breaks off from that of early Jewish and first-century Christian views. In the Old Testament, an absolute distinction is maintained between the creator God and his creation: 'I am the Lord, the maker of all things, who alone stretched out the heavens, who spread out the earth by myself...' (Isa. 44: 24). In the New Testament, Jesus alone among human beings stands with his Father on the divine side of the God–creation divide. On the other hand, Gnostic thinkers tended to see the spirit which was a part of the human person by nature as at the same time a flash of divine light: 'Jesus said, "That which you have will save you when you bring it forth from yourselves. That which you do not have within you will kill you if you do not have it within you." ' (*Gospel of Thomas*, § 70).[15] But when Jesus asks the disciples to stand before him in this scene in the *Gospel of Judas*, their divine 'selves' are too diluted by their ignorance to be up to the task.

Judas, however, is strong enough. Some eminent Gnosticism scholars have argued that even in his own Gospel Judas is simply a demonic and doomed figure. The first piece of evidence to qualify this view is Judas's strength in standing before Jesus. He is already marked out as destined for heavenly rule: those who are heading for this paradise are characterized as 'strong and holy' on the next page of the codex (p. 36).

Judas also differs from the other disciples in that he alone knows the truth—although it is a truth which might sound to us like something from a science fiction novel: 'you have come from the immortal aeon of Barbelo'. 'Aeon' is in one respect a fairly common word in antiquity, with a meaning similar to the English 'aeon'. But, as was mentioned in Chapter 3, in Gnostic literature the term comes to have a technical meaning. The difficulty in defining it comes from the fact that it refers both to a heavenly realm and at the same time to a sentient divine personage.

Barbelo is generally a female divinity (although at a deeper level, an androgynous one) in Gnostic thought, and she is *la* Barbelo in this passage of the *Gospel of Judas* as well—the feminine form of the definite article is used for her here. Her curriculum vitae consists of numerous epithets and titles in Gnostic literature, including 'Protennoia' (the 'first thought' of the unknown God), 'ineffable silence', and 'ineffable, incorruptible, immeasurable, inconceivable'. She can also be described as the 'triple power', 'male-virgin', and 'shadow of the holy father'.[16] In fact, in the hierarchy of Gnostic divinities she is generally second only to the Great Invisible Spirit himself.

But it is not just that Jesus has come from the aeon of Barbelo. He is apparently despatched from there by this supreme Great Invisible Spirit. Here, then, the mistake of the other disciples is clear to see: they thought that the true god was the one worshiped in their 'eucharist', but according to Judas's statement here the highest divinity is completely ineffable and incomprehensible.

Jesus, knowing that Judas was also pondering other exalted things, said to him, 'Separate yourself from them. I will speak to you the mysteries of the Kingdom, not so that you might enter it, but so you will grieve greatly. <36> For another will

come to your place so that the twelve [disciples] might again be complete in their god.'

And Judas said to him, 'When will you tell me these things and when will the great day of the light of the generation dawn... ...?' But when he said these things, Jesus left him.

This clearly calls to mind the events at the beginning of the Acts of the Apostles which we examined in Chapter 2: Judas's apostasy and death, and then the divine choice of who will replace him. In the New Testament, Judas is guilty of having abandoned Jesus and the disciples to go his own way, hence the need for a new apostle. But in the *Gospel of Judas*, by contrast, Judas is told by Jesus to remove himself from the apostolic group ('separate yourself'). Judas leaves the apostolate, which—Jesus says in rather disparaging tones—will be made up to twelve again for the benefit of the disciples' god. This replacement is perhaps because he is the Old Testament God, the god who chose the twelve sons of Jacob to be the patriarchs of the twelve tribes of Israel, and the twelve disciples of Jesus to represent a renewed Israel: in other words, this god is being faintly mocked for having a fixation with the number twelve. For now, Judas is being portrayed in a positive light: Jesus talks to Judas of the disciples and 'their' (i.e. not Jesus' or Judas's) god.

This attention to making up the number to twelve (not the focus in Acts) may also allude to the aeon-myth, which in Chapter 3 we saw was attributed to the Gnostics by the Church Fathers. The reconstitution of the twelve in the *Gospel of Judas* might in some way mirror the restoration of Sophia, after her defection, to her place as the last of the twelve aeons. The excerpt cited here refers to Judas's *grief* (a major theme associated with Sophia's fall) which results from another disciple replacing him. Furthermore, Jesus stresses that Judas cannot yet enter the Kingdom.

On the other hand, Judas—later to be called 'the thirteenth'—does not fit into this group any more. He is to stand aside from the other disciples and receive private revelations. The *Gospel of Thomas* again provides an instance of another author who thought along the same lines:

And Jesus took him [i.e. Thomas] and withdrew, and said three words to him. When Thomas came back to his companions, they asked him, 'What did Jesus say to you?' Thomas said to them, 'If I tell you one of the words which he spoke to me, you would pick up stones and throw them at me. But fire would come out of the stones and burn you.' (*Gospel of Thomas*, § 13)[17]

In the case of Judas, the revelation is at this point rather brief, but, as we have said, the second half of the document takes up the 'mysteries of the Kingdom' which Jesus is going to impart to Judas.

Day 2: Jesus Speaks Incomprehensible Mysteries
When it was morning, he appeared to his disciples.

And they said to him, 'Master, where did you go? What did you do when you left us?'

Jesus said to them, 'I went to another great generation, which is holy.'

His disciples said to him, 'Lord, what is the great generation which is exalted over us and holy and not now in these aeons?'

And when Jesus heard these things, he laughed. He said to them, 'Why are you pondering in your hearts concerning the generation which is strong and holy? <37> Truly [I] say to you, [no-]one born [of] this aeon will see that [generation]. No army of star-angels will rule over that generation.

Nor will anyone born of mortal man be able to accompany it. For that generation does not come forth ... ... which has come into being. ... ... The generation of men in your midst is from the generation of humanity (almost one line missing) **power ... ... other powers ... ... as you are kings among [them].' When [his] disciples heard these things, they each were disturbed in [their] spirits and were not able to say anything.**

The reader can to some extent sympathize with the disciples' disorientation at Jesus' sudden appearances and disappearances in the *Gospel of Judas*. Here Jesus has been away visiting a different dimension, whose denizens are the 'great generation' which is 'strong and holy'. We saw above Jesus' declaration to the disciples (on 'day 1') that *no generation among the men who are in your midst will know me*: in contrast there is another group which truly belongs to him—the 'immortal generation of Seth' as they are called in the second part of the *Gospel of Judas*. This time, Jesus does seem to be laughing more directly *at* the disciples, as is implied by the way he goes on to ask why they are even bothering to think about the blessed generation.

That generation will not only be forever alien to the disciples, their 'aeon', and to mortal humanity in general; these holy ones will also be superior to, or at least invulnerable to, the armies of 'star-angels'. Stars and angels have a long history of being associated with one another in the Ancient Near East and in Jewish apocalyptic writings, and the close correlation between them survives into Gnostic literature in the opening statement of *The Testimony of Truth*:

I will speak to those who know to hear not with the ears of the body but with the ears of the mind. For many have sought after the truth and have not been able to find it; because the old leaven of the Pharisees and the scribes of the Law has taken control of them. And the leaven is the false desire of the angels and the demons and the stars. The Pharisees and the Scribes are those who belong to the archons with authority over them.[18]

This statement confirms the picture that will become apparent in the *Gospel of Judas*: that in the main, these star-angels are negative figures—heavenly powers which have gone astray and which hold humanity in thrall in some way (see pp. 46 and 55 of the codex). But those belonging to the holy generation are decidedly not 'the stars' tennis-balls, struck and banded which way please them', as Bosola puts it in *The Duchess of Malfi* (V.iv.54–5).

Despite the important themes in this passage, the overall impression is of Jesus blinding the disciples with science, confirming them in the 'stupidity' of day 1. They are left bewildered and speechless, as is sometimes the case in the New Testament Gospels (e.g. Mark 9: 32). And our situation is even worse than that of the disciples because of the gaps in the manuscript.

Day 3: The Temple Vision
Jesus came to them on another day and they said to him, 'Master, we have seen you in a [vision]. For we saw great dreams in this past night.'

[He said,] 'Why have … … you have hidden yourselves?'

<38> And they [said], 'We have seen a great house with a great altar in it, and twelve men (who, we think, are priests), and a name. There is a crowd waiting at that altar for the priests [to come] out [and conduct] the service. And we were also waiting.'

[Jesus said], 'What were [the priests] like?'

[They said], 'Some ... ... two weeks. [Others] sacrifice their own children, others their wives as they bless and are humiliated by each other. Others sleep with men. Others do murderous deeds. Still others commit a multitude of sins and transgressions. But the men who stand at the altar call upon your [name] <39> and as they are engaged in all the deeds of their slaughter, the [altar] fills up.' And after they said these things, they fell silent, as they were troubled.

Jesus said to them, 'Why have you become troubled? Truly, I say to you, all the priests who were standing at that altar call upon my name. Again I say to you, my name has been written upon [this house] for the generations of stars by the generations of men. But they have shamefully planted fruitless trees in my name.'

Jesus said to them, '*You* are those offering services at the altar which you saw. That is the god whom you serve, and the twelve men whom you saw are you yourselves. And as for the animals which are brought as the sacrifices which you saw, they are the multitude which you deceive <40> at that altar ... will arise and this is how he will treat my name. And the generations of the 'pious' will attend him. After him, another man—one of the adulterers—will arise. And another, one of those who kill children, will arise, and another, one of those who sleep with men, and from those who fast, and the rest of those of impurity, lawlessness, and error. And as for those who say, 'we are like angels'—they are stars which have completely died out. For they have said to the generations of men, 'behold, God accepts your sacrifices from the priest'— who is the minister of error. But the Lord who commands is the one who is Lord over the all. On the last day they will be found guilty.'

<41> Jesus said to them, 'Cease your sacrificing (2 lines mostly missing)...upon the altar, since they are above your stars and your angels which have already died out there. So let them...in your presence and go....'

The final nail in the coffin of the disciples is that they have seen in a vision twelve priests of despicable corruption, standing by the carcases of their sacrificial victims, only to be told by Jesus that they, the disciples, are those very priests.[19] The victims symbolically refer to the simple masses who perish for lack of knowledge, led astray by the disciple-priests. Jesus continues to distance himself from their god, whom we already know from page 34 in the codex to be a figure of fun as far as Jesus is concerned.

We will see in Chapter 6 how this passage contributes usefully to the discussion of when the *Gospel of Judas* was composed. But another point on which this segment sheds light is the practice of mudslinging in antiquity. 'Orthodox' and 'Gnostic' alike apparently accused each other of immorality, and the pagans joined in as well. The vision here implies that our author and his circle were probably not 'Gnostic libertines'. In fact, the author here is returning the complement, as Marvin Meyer has already said, in paying the orthodox back with the kinds of accusations that were levelled at a number of Gnostics.[20]

In this section, as well, our author shows no sympathy for traditional Christian piety: having rejected the eucharist at the beginning of the document, Jesus appears in his interpretation of this temple vision to have no truck with the common Jewish and Christian practice of fasting, and in a postscript to his interpretation of the disciples' vision, reiterates his condemnation of the eucharist.

Translation and Interpretation

[Sections of very fragmentary text]

(approx. 16 lines missing) **generations...A baker is not able to feed all creation** <42> **which is under** [heaven]. **And ... ...them ... ...and ... ...us and ... .**

Jesus said to them, 'Cease your contention with me. Each one of you has his star and ...' (approx. 17 lines missing) <43> 'In (most of line missing) he did not come to ... ...of the spring of the tree of (most of line missing) of this aeon ... ...after time (most of line missing). But it came to water the paradise of God, and the generation which will endure, because...will not defile the...of that generation. But...is from eternity to eternity.'

It has been estimated that the *Gospel of Judas* as we have it represents approximately 85–90 per cent of the original text, and so we do have a good idea of what the document is about and the thought-world from which it derives.[21] What these big gaps in the manuscript mean, however, is that it is much more difficult to be sure of any form of 'structure' which the original might have had. It is possible that—in line with the Prologue—there was originally one scene for each day of that week leading up to the third day before Passover: the first three scenes which we have identified above take place on three different days. Scholars have speculated on what might have been mentioned in some of these gaps, but it is impossible to have any real idea of their content.

In amongst the gaps, the first sentence seems to be a proverb of some sort. Then on page 42 of the manuscript there is a comment by Jesus about the disciples each having a corresponding star—a theme evident in Plato (where every person has a companion star) and which bears comparison with the

Gnostic idea we have seen reported by the Church Fathers in which the disciples embody the twelve aeons in some way.[22] Finally, there is a section which is clearly about the Garden of Eden: the Coptic word *paradeisos*, borrowed from the Greek, which is borrowed from the Persian, can mean either 'paradise' or 'garden'. Eden is of course famous for its trees, and the watering of the paradise/garden in this section is another allusion to it: 'A river flowed out of Eden to water the garden, and from there it was divided and became four rivers' (Gen. 2: 10).

Conclusion to Part I
In sum, then, the polemic against the 'Great Church' includes the following elements:

Day 1

— Jesus laughing at the disciples' eucharist
— the reason for the laughter—Jesus rejecting the disciples' god
— the disciples' inability to stand in Jesus' spiritual presence
— the truth about Jesus' identity shown to be known only to Judas

Day 2

— the contrast between the disciples and the holy generation

Day 3

— the picture of the disciples as terrible sinners.

In sum, then, the apostles who are the basis of the Church are recast as villains. The version of events here is a dramatic parody of the account in the four New Testament Gospels, where of course Judas is unique among the disciples as Jesus' betrayer. In the *Gospel of Judas*, it is the majority, the eleven (later to be made up to twelve again), who are portrayed as a false foundation for the mainstream Church—this Church and its gospels are the real target of our author. Judas, however, has been asked by Jesus to separate himself from the disciples. Unlike these others who are steeped in invincible ignorance, Judas is to be the sole, privileged recipient of divine revelation, of true heavenly *gnōsis*. This is to be the main theme of the second part of the work.

Part II: The Revelation to Judas
There are two major themes in this second half of the work: the beginning, i.e. creation, and the end, or consummation of all things. The creation account is a monologue by Jesus and is sandwiched between two blocks of dialogue which are focused on the end of time. The way the text is structured in the translation below is partly guesswork, given that the text is full of holes. But, as it stands, the text can be organized roughly as follows:

A. Dialogue on the Hereafter

    1. The Holy Generation and the Rest
    2. Judas's Temple Vision
    3. Judas's Destiny

B. Jesus' Account of the Creations

Introduction

    1. The Clouds, Autogenes, and his Angels
    2. Creation of the Aeons, Luminaries, and Angels
    3. Creation of the Generation of Seth

4. The Emergence of the Cosmos
5. Creation of the Rulers of the Underworld
6. The Creation of Adam and Eve

Concluding Dialogue on Creation

C. Dialogue on the Hereafter (continued)

4. The Destiny of the Cosmos
5. Judas's Destiny

These are followed by the account of Judas handing Jesus over to the Jewish authorities.

Dialogue on the Hereafter

1. The Holy Generation and the Rest
Judas said to [him], 'Rabbi, what is the fruit which this generation has?'

Jesus said, 'The souls of every generation of man will die. But as for them (i.e. the holy generation), when the time of the kingdom is fulfilled and the spirit separates from them, their bodies will die, but their souls will be made alive and will be raised up.'

After the fragmentary top of the page, the theme of this question and answer is obviously the personal immortality which the blessed generation will experience. This passage is illuminated by the later discussion on page 53 of the codex which talks about the 'spirits of man' being on short-term loan—hence the reference here to the spirit separating from the body. This much appears to be true for everyone. But we already know that there is a fundamental divide within humanity: ordinary human beings have bodies and souls both of which die; the

Gnostic, however, has a soul which will be re-energized and given a resurrection. On the other hand, as one would expect in a Gnostic text, the physical body has no future—a physical resurrection would hold absolutely no interest for Gnostics, who regarded the body as excess baggage at best, but more often as something along the lines of 'the tomb', or 'the fetter of oblivion'.[23] It is only the *souls* of this holy generation which are resurrected.

Judas said, 'What then will become of the rest of the generations of men?'

Jesus said, 'It is impossible <44> to plant on a rock and then
reap fruit. This is how ... ... of the generation ... with corruptible Sophia ... the hand which created mortal men whose souls
go up to the aeons above. Truly I say to you, ' ... ... [nor] angel,
[nor] power will be able to see those ... These who ... ... the
holy generation ... them.'

When Jesus had said these things, he went away.

Again, the holes in the manuscript invite a certain amount of guesswork. Having discussed the holy generation, Judas is now interested in the rest of humanity, who are described by Jesus in terms reminiscent of the New Testament 'parable of the sower'—like the seed which 'fell on rocky ground'.[24] Members of the rest of humanity are also associated with 'corruptible Sophia', an apparently strange designation for Lady Wisdom, but understandable against the background of Gnostic texts which (as we saw in Chapter 3) saw Sophia as having a split personality. She could be both the higher, perfect Sophia (who is sometimes also identified with Barbelo), and the Sophia in evidence here: the lady of ill-repute who overreached herself without permission and gave birth to imperfect creations. One scholar has made the intriguing suggestion that in the reference to the rock as useless and unproductive there is a possible allusion to Peter—in the New Testament the 'rock' of the early Church.[25]

All this is of course in contrast to the people described in the previous snippet: the perfect, holy generation. After these enigmatic utterances, we again see Jesus leaving the stage, as he did at the end of the scene on day 1.

2. Judas's Temple Vision

Judas said, 'Master, just as you have listened to all of them, listen also to me. For I have seen a great vision.'

But when Jesus heard this, he laughed and said to him, 'Why do you struggle so, O thirteenth spirit? But speak, and I will be patient with you.'

Judas said to him, 'I saw myself in the vision, and the twelve disciples throwing stones at me. They were <45> pursuing [me]...And I went again to the place......after you. I saw [a house]...and its measurements my eyes would not be able [to measure]. And some great men were surrounding it and that house had a roof of herbs. And in the middle of the house was (approx. two lines mostly missing). Master, receive me in with these men.'

[Jesus] answered and said, 'Your star has deceived you, O Judas. No progeny of any mortal man is worthy to enter into the house which you saw, for that place is kept for the holy ones, the place where Sun and Moon will not have dominion, nor will the Evil One.[26] But they (i.e. 'the holy ones') will stand for all time in the aeon with the holy angels. Behold, I have spoken to you the mysteries of the Kingdom. <46> And I have taught you [about the] deception of the stars, and … twelve[27] … (almost one line missing) **over the twelve aeons.'**

Jesus responds to Judas's initial question with some slight exasperation. Nevertheless, he expresses willingness, albeit somewhat reluctantly, to listen to the 'thirteenth spirit'—thirteenth because he has been removed from (and elevated over) the twelve disciples, and 'spirit' because this is the only component of his being which is ultimately of any significance.

Judas's reference to the great men surrounding this house and to the roof of grass is rather unusual. The oversized men may be angels, though their height is perhaps merely part of the symbolism in keeping with the great size of the building. Although the precise meaning of the imagery is obscure, what is clear is that the house which Judas has seen in his vision represents the paradise where the holy generation will in the end dwell with the angels; the imagery of the awesome proportions of the building is balanced by the grass roof, which conjures up a sense of lush, paradisal fruitfulness as well. It rather resembles the Hanging Gardens of Babylon, with their massive walls and towers combined with cultivated terrace-roofs.[28] This strikes the same balance as the New Testament book of Revelation, which portrays heaven both as a new Jerusalem, a city, but also as a new Garden of Eden.

According to Jesus' reply on hearing the report of the vision, Judas has not yet been perfected: his star has deceived him and misled him into thinking that he is ready to enter paradise. In fact, only the divine immortals, and presumably the spiritual souls of the holy generation, can go into the place where no heavenly powers (such as Sun and Moon mentioned in the vision) will be in control: this fits with the Gnostic theme, which we will discuss later, of being free from rule. Judas will belong to this generation, but he must progress to perfect knowledge, and by the end of Jesus' response here, Judas has taken an important step forward in understanding—he has heard the mysteries of the kingdom. But he still has some way to go.

3. Judas's Destiny

Judas said, 'Master, surely my seed will never submit to the archons?'

Jesus answered and said to him, 'Come, and I will ... [you] (two lines almost completely missing) but you will grieve greatly as you see the kingdom with all its generation.'

When Judas had heard these things, he said to Jesus, 'What is the benefit which I have received as a result of you setting me apart for that generation?'

Jesus answered and said, 'You will become the thirteenth. You will be cursed by the rest of the generations, but you will rule over them. In those last days they will {...?} you and that you might not (?) ascend to the <47> holy generation.'

The first question and answer here concerns the 'archons', a common feature of Gnostic systems: these are heavenly authorities who exercise a negative influence over the government of the cosmos (like the stars, as we have seen), often attempting to prevent the soul from ascending to its destined heavenly rest. To 'submit to the archons', as Judas puts it, would be to fall under the same dominion as the doomed mass of unredeemed humanity, as opposed to being part of the 'indomitable race' (as it is described on page 53) to which Judas really belongs.

Judas's second question focuses pragmatically on the benefits he will receive. Some have linked Judas's enquiry, 'What is the benefit...?' with a question by Judas's namesake *Judah* in the book of Genesis, but this is unlikely to be right.[29] Jesus' answer to the question is a promise to Judas that he is to stand apart from the apostolic circle (the twelve) and as a result be rejected by everyone (this presumably refers to Judas's reputation in the wider Church at the time, as we saw reflected in the New Testament, the Apostolic Fathers, and the apocryphal literature of the second century CE). Judas's grief will only be temporary, however. He will be superior to the other disciples as his soul perhaps makes its heavenly journey to what has just been pictured as the giant garden-roofed house. The language here has been much disputed by scholars, but may well be a reference to his future existence with the holy generation.[30] The interpretation is extremely difficult here, however, because of a scribal error at the beginning of the line in question: instead of a reference to Judas's ascent, the reference may be to the attempt of 'the rest' to *prevent* that ascent; others take it as evidence that Judas will *not* ascend.

With the present dialogue about the end-times events complete, the *Gospel of Judas* moves into monologue form, and addresses the beginnings—the events of creation.

Jesus' Account of the Creations

A great deal of emphasis has been placed in the literature so far on the *Gospel of Judas* on the events leading up to the betrayal of Jesus: the *Gospel of Judas* sees a need to explain what goes on in that week leading up to when the New Testament accounts begin their description of the arrest, trial, and crucifixion of Jesus.

Just as important in the *Gospel of Judas*, however, is the way the work supplements another biblical account: the opening chapters of Genesis. Writing a revised version of the creation story in these chapters seems to have been a favourite indoor sport for Gnostics. The principal reason for a Gnostic wanting to rewrite Genesis is that it begins with God making the heavens and the earth, and Adam and Eve, and so on. But for the author of the *Gospel of Judas*, this rushes far too quickly into the creation of the physical world: as every good Platonist knows, a heavenly blueprint of the cosmos is required before the physical world can then be based upon it.

In several of his works, the Greek philosopher Plato (*c*.427–347 BCE) discusses his theory of 'Forms' which are the eternal essences of which everything in the tangible world is only an imperfect copy. While the physical world is perceptible by the senses, only the mind or the soul can grasp these Forms. As Plato puts it in the *Timaeus*:

It must be agreed that there exists, first, the self-identical Form, uncreated and indestructible, which neither receives to itself anything else from anywhere else, nor passes into anything else in any direction. It is invisible, and imperceptible to the other senses; thought alone is privileged to have access to it.

Second, having the same name and resembling it, is the perceptible, created, always changing, coming into being in a particular place and passing away from that place. It is apprehended by opinion with perception. (Plato, *Timaeus*, 52A)

Because Plato regards these Forms as eternal and self-existent, they are almost certainly not in his view created by God. There is, nevertheless, a 'Demiurge'—the creator-deity—who is involved in giving order to the visible world.

The Jewish philosopher Philo of Alexandria (1st century CE) does think in terms of two realms, as per Timaeus, but regards both as created by the God of the Bible:

For God, as he is God, understood in advance that a fine copy could never come into being without a fine pattern. Nor would anything in the perceptible sphere be faultless which was not constructed in accordance with the archetype and intelligible idea. Intending, then, to create the visible world, he first formed the intelligible world, so that, making use of the incorporeal and god-like pattern, he then made the physical, the newer being the reflection of the older, the former incorporating such perceptible kinds as were intelligible in the latter. (Philo, *On the Creation of the World*, § 16)

Philo goes on to draw an analogy with someone wanting to build a city: first, the king or governor will commission a trained architect. This architect will first conceive in his mind a plan for the city, then go on to have it built. The *Gospel of Judas* is less positive about the material world but does at least agree with Philo that the heavenly world is created first, after which the earthly copies come into existence as reflections of it.

Introduction

Jesus said, '[Come], and I will teach you about (almost one line missing) **which no man will see. For a great, limitless aeon exists, whose measure no generation of angels has seen. In it is [the] Great and Invisible Spirit, "whom no angel's eye has seen; nor has the thought of a mind received it; nor has it been called by any name." '**

This section on creation, which will perfect Judas's knowledge, is introduced with a formula common in Gnostic texts: the revelation of that which no eye has seen, no ear has heard, and has never before entered the human mind. This formula uses elements from the Old Testament book of Isaiah, but is first found in the mid-first century in the apostle Paul and in a Jewish work from roughly the same time, the *Biblical Antiquities*.[31]

The subject matter of this revelation is the limitless aeon, or Great Invisible Spirit, a figure who is standard fare in the Gnostic literature from Nag Hammadi, often as the supreme God above all the others. In fact, the *Apocryphon of John*, among other texts, argues that he should not be called a god at all, because he is greater than that title implies: he can only really be described in negative terms, as unsearchable, ineffable, unnameable, immeasurable, and the like.[32] He is pictured there, however, as 'pure light', and it is as a 'cloud of light' that he (or the aeon in which he resides) comes on the scene here in the *Gospel of Judas*.

1. The Clouds, Autogenes, and his Angels

And there appeared in that place a cloud of light.

And he said, 'Let there be an angel to attend me.' And there came forth from the cloud a great angel, Autogenes the god of light. And another four angels came into being for his sake, from another cloud. And they came into being to attend Autogenes the angel.

So this 'cloud of light', the first speaker in the drama of creation here, is almost certainly identified in some way with the Great Invisible Spirit—a being of pure light at the top of, or simply altogether beyond, the heavenly Gnostic bureaucracy (see Fig. 4.1). The next level down is occupied by Autogenes (literally, 'self-Generated') who, although an angelic figure, is a great angel, of a very different order of being from the four angels from the lesser cloud who serve him.[33] These initial events of creation in the account here in fact trigger a succession

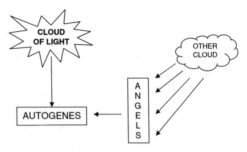

Figure 4.1. Diagrammatic Representation of the Events of the Creation in the *Gospel of Judas.*

of further creations: Autogenes and his minions will themselves generate additional entities.

2. Creation of the Aeons, Luminaries, and Ministering Angels
And Autogenes said, <48> 'Let [Adamas ?] come into being'. And there came into being…… And he made the first luminary to rule over him. And he said, 'Let some angels come into being to minister to him.' And tens of thousands without number came into being.

And he said, 'Let an aeon of light come into being.' And he came into being, and Autogenes created the second luminary to rule over him, with tens of thousands of innumerable angels for his service.

And thus he created the rest of the aeons of light, and he caused them (i.e. the luminaries) to rule over them, and he created for them tens of thousands of innumerable angels for their service.

In addition to Autogenes and his four angels from the beginnings of creation, we now have a series of aeons, each of whom is governed by a luminary and served by lesser angels.

Unfortunately, the first entity to come into being is missing from the manuscript, though it is probably Adamas (the divine, heavenly prototype of Adam): he will be prominent in the next section. Other Gnostic works designate Autogenes as the father or creator of Adamas: 'With all these thus established, Autogenes produces in addition a perfect and true man, whom they also call Adamas, since neither he nor those from whom he came have ever been conquered' (Irenaeus, *Against Heresies*, 1.29.3). This reference to Adamas being 'unconquerable' probably shows that his name derives not only from his being the heavenly prototype of the biblical Adam; *adamas* is also the Greek word for 'unconquerable' or 'unbreakable' (as in the English, 'adamant', 'adamantine', etc.).

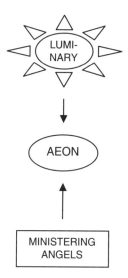

Figure 4.2. Aeons, Luminaries, and Ministering Angels. (A luminary rules over each aeon, and each aeon is served by angels.)

The first two stages of Autogenes's creative activity seem to be modelled upon the account of God creating the principal luminaries (the sun and the moon) in Genesis:

God made two great luminaries, the greater luminary to rule the day and the smaller luminary to rule the night; and he made the stars. God placed them in the firmament of heaven to give light on the earth, to rule the day and the night, and to separate light from darkness. (Gen. 1: 16–18)

In the version of events in the *Gospel of Judas*, there is a clear hierarchy with luminaries above the aeons, reflecting *mutatis mutandis* this account in Genesis. At the lowest level in this particular Gnostic system are the ministering angels, who serve the aeons.

3. Creation of the Generation of Seth

And Adamas was in that first cloud of light which no angel among all those who are called gods has seen. And he <49> {And} (almost whole line missing) that (almost whole line missing) the image (almost whole line missing) and according to the likeness of [this] angel. He revealed the incorruptible [generation] of Seth ... ... the twelve ... ... twenty four ... ...

He revealed seventy-two luminaries in the incorruptible generation in the will of the Spirit.

And the seventy-two luminaries revealed 360 luminaries in the incorruptible generation in the will of the Spirit, so that their number might be five for each one.

And their father is the twelve aeons of the twelve luminaries. And there are six heavens per aeon so that there might be seventy-two heavens for the seventy-two luminaries, and for each one <50> [of them, five] firmaments, [so that there might be] three hundred and sixty [firmaments.]

We know from elsewhere that Adamas's role consists in revealing eternal beings, and here he causes the whole generation of Gnostic spirits to appear (see Fig. 4.2), the first of which is Seth—again, not the biblical Seth strictly speaking, but his heavenly Spirit-prototype.[34] This Seth figure is the father of the 'holy generation' (hence 'their father' above) referred to in the *Gospel of Judas*, and is in fact mentioned a great many times in Gnostic writings in this role. Marvin Meyer's essay in the National Geographic volume gives a very helpful overview of 'Sethian Gnosticism', as the movement associated with this body of literature is often called.[35]

This section also advances the creation account by presenting each aeon with six heavens (for a total of seventy-two heavens). Adamas then creates seventy-two luminaries, which in turn create 360 more (but which are presumably lesser lights than their seventy-two creators). Each of these greater luminaries and the heavens twinned with them then receives five 'firmaments'. The firmament in biblical tradition is the canopy of heaven which separates the waters above from the earth, so even though these firmaments are probably conceptualized differently here, five for each heaven, or luminary, seems quite excessive—a little like a person carrying five umbrellas. But the point here is that the realms created by Autogenes and Adamas are a magnificently fecund arrangement, one whose complexity and obscurity would have been meat and drink to the Gnostic believer.

4. *The Emergence of the Cosmos*

[They] were given authority and a [great] army of [innumerable] angels, for glorification and service, and then virgin spirits for the glorification and [service] of all the aeons and the heavens and their firmaments. But the host of those immortals is called 'Cosmos', that is, 'corruption', by the Father and the seventy-two luminaries who are with Autogenes and his seventy-two aeons.

As we have noted, it is ministering angels and spirits who are at the bottom of the social ladder in this Gnostic system, hence perhaps the snobbery of the Father (the supreme divinity) and Autogenes designating the angels and spirits here as constituting *Cosmos* ('world') or 'corruption'. Since this 'cosmos' is almost certainly the archetype of the *physical* world, this introduces what for many scholars is one of the key components of Gnosticism—a very negative valuation of the material creation. In the biblical scheme, the created world is initially 'good' before it is corrupted by death and decay.[36] In the *Gospel of Judas* here, however, the physical world is apparently this way from the outset, reflecting the likeness of its pre-existent counterpart, Cosmos.

It is a little surprising that midway through the account of apparently powerful and pure ('virgin') spirits we are suddenly told that they constitute the corrupted world. The reason for this sudden non sequitur is probably lost to us, as it seems to arise from the fact that this whole section only 'summarises in compressed form' an earlier source on which it is drawing.[37] This explanation is probably supported by the same literary phenomenon in a work from Nag Hammadi, *Eugnostos the Blessed*. Here in the midst of a creation account whose components seem on the surface to be unimpeachable, thus far, we read the following:

When the firmaments were completed, they were called the three hundred and sixty heavens, after the name of the heavens which were before them. And all these were complete and good. And in this way the deficiency of femaleness appeared.[38]

Again, the reason for the transition from perfection to the appearance of what is defective or corrupt in nature is unclear. The best guess for this in the *Gospel of Judas* is probably simply that we are by now a number of stages removed from the light-cloud and Autogenes. If the emanations from the luminous cloud, the Great Invisible Spirit, have been getting progressively distant from him/it, eventually the light is so diluted that the archetype of the corrupt world comes into being.

In that place (i.e. 'Cosmos'), **the first man appeared with his incorruptible powers. The aeon who appeared with his generation is that which contained the cloud of knowledge and the angel called** <51> **El** (almost whole line missing) **with** (almost whole line missing) **aeon** (almost whole line missing).

This heavenly archetype of the cosmos then becomes the sphere in which Adamas is to dwell: he is almost certainly this first man who boasts incorruptible powers (unlike the earthly Adam, the corruptible man *par excellence*). We have already encountered Adamas as the one who revealed the immortal generation of his son, Seth, hence the reference to the first man and his generation. Adamas's generation here—that is, Seth and everyone following him—is accompanied by an aeon containing an angel called by the Hebrew word for 'god', and the cloud of knowledge.

'Knowledge' (*gnōsis*) here is the all-important concept in much of this kind of literature, and this is particularly clear in the *Gospel of Judas* as we have seen from both the prologue and the way Jesus has been instructing Judas. The fact that the cloud containing it accompanies the generation of Seth ensures their salvation.

5. *Creation of the Rulers of the Underworld*

After these things ... said, 'Let twelve angels come into being, [to] rule over chaos and [Hades].' And, behold, an [angel] appeared out of the cloud with his face pouring forth fire. His appearance was polluted with blood, and his name was 'Nebro', which interpreted means 'apostate'; others say, 'Yaldabaoth'. And, again, another angel came forth from the cloud—Saklas. Therefore Nebro created six angels for assistance, as did Saklas. And so they begat the twelve angels in the heavens, and a portion in the heavens was taken for each one.

The next stage, then, is the creation of those who are to rule chaos and the underworld—a function of ambiguous status. Milton's Satan in *Paradise Lost* made a virtue out of what he saw as a necessity: 'Better to reign in hell, than serve in heav'n' (Book I, l. 263). In Homer's *Odyssey*, on the other hand, Achilles takes a rather different view: 'I would rather be a farm-labourer to another, to some portionless man of no great substance, than be lord of all the dead in their ruin' (*Odyssey*, 11.489–91). Perhaps the most pithy remark on the subject comes in the Old Testament book of Ecclesiastes: 'better a living dog than a dead lion' (Eccles. 9: 4). In any case, the job of creating these infernal monarchs is assigned to Nebro and Saklas, two of the more unsavoury deities in the Gnostic pantheon.

'Nebro' is a shortened form of the name Nebrod or Nebrodes, a figure better known by the Hebrew spelling of his name: Nimrod, 'mighty hunter before the Lord' (Gen. 10: 9). In the book of Genesis, he is an ancient hero, the King of Babel who then went on to build the city of Nineveh. Modern scholars have speculated endlessly over how we should understand the origins of this enigmatic figure, and in fact the speculation was just as rampant in antiquity. Other Jews and Christians filled in the gaps as our author does in the *Gospel of Judas*: by making Nimrod into a semi-divine figure, and exploring his dark side through, among other things, etymology. Philo of Alexandria (in the first century CE) has the first stab at an explanation of the name: 'his name means "desertion" ' (*On the Giants*, 66).

This comes from seeing the name as derived from the Hebrew *marad*, 'to rebel', and is reinforced by Nimrod's reputation for having led people astray from God: being a *hunter*, he was in the habit of ensnaring people. The closest parallel of all to our passage here, however, is in the Church Father Jerome (331–420 CE) in his *Book of the Interpretation of Hebrew Names*: Nimrod there means 'apostate', as well as 'tyrant, fugitive, transgressor'.[39]

In Nag Hammadi texts such as the *Gospel of the Egyptians*, Nimrod again accompanies Saklas in creation, and is named Nebruel (= 'Nebro' + the divine name 'El'). Reasons for his being covered in blood in the *Gospel of Judas* may be because he is associated with the biblical god who required sacrifices, or simply because he is frequently engaged in the gory occupation of hunting.[40]

Unlike many of the extremely abstract deities in Gnostic texts, Yaldabaoth is painted very vividly (the *Apocryphon of John* has one of the most extensive descriptions). He is the offspring of Sophia, illegitimate, as we have already seen, because he was formed when she wanted to reproduce her image without the will of her male consort, the Spirit. The monstrosity that resulted appeared like a snake with the face of a lion (although he could also change his face whenever he wanted), with eyes flashing like the fires of lightning, as similarly here in the *Gospel of Judas*. He flees from his mother and grows in strength such that he is able eventually to create the authorities who reign over the underworld. He is portrayed as the creator of Adam, although in the *Gospel of Judas* this part of his characterization is given to Saklas.

The name of Saklas, or Sakla, as he is also called, is derived from the Aramaic *sakla*, meaning 'foolish', or 'fool'. Closely associated with the 'satan' of the biblical tradition, he is in the snappily titled *Trimorphic Protennoia* ...

the great demon who rules over the bottom of the underworld and chaos. He has neither form nor completeness, but has the form of the glory of those who are born in darkness. And he is called 'Saklas', that is 'Samael', or 'Yaltabaoth' ... [41]

So the two figures of Saklas and Nebro-Yaldabaoth are very closely related: here and in other texts as well they are regarded as the same character.[42] The reason for Saklas getting his name 'fool' is quite specific. His folly consists in his claim that he is the sole or at least supreme divinity: 'I am God and there is no other God besides me'.[43] So there is an identification here between Saklas and the biblical God, who says the same thing in the Old Testament book of Isaiah (Isa. 43: 12 + 44: 6).

After Nebro-Yaldabaoth and Saklas have each created their six angelic assistants, these are given places in heaven.

And the twelve archons said to the twelve angels, 'Let each one of you' <52> (almost whole line missing) **and they** (almost whole line missing) **generation** (almost whole line missing) ... **angel.**

The first is ... who is called 'Christ'.
The [second] is Harmathoth, who (almost whole line missing).
The third is Galila.
The fourth is Yobel.
The fifth is Adonaios.
These are the five who ruled over the underworld, and formerly over chaos.

After the fragmentary beginning, we have the five rulers who apparently first ruled over the chaos of the beginning of creation, and were also to govern the realm of the dead. The number five comes about because the twelve angels created by Nebro and Saklas are divided in Gnostic tradition (in the *Apocryphon of John*, for example) into two groups: seven to reign over part or parts of heaven and the remaining five to take charge of the underworld.[44] Whether this is simply assumed by our author in his compressed account, or was described in the (now lost) lines at the top of page 52 is unclear: either way, we only have the five subterranean governors before us.

1. The distinction between Jesus and 'Christ' as different figures is actually quite common in Gnostic literature. In the course of the narratives and dialogues in the *Gospel of Judas*, Jesus is always called just 'Jesus', whereas 'Christ' may have had associations of Jewish messiahship (Christ being simply the Greek form of the Hebrew Messiah) which Gnostic tradition would rather do without.

2. Harmathoth is almost certainly a combination of the Greek god *Hermes* and the Egyptian *Thoth*, names which refer to the same deity: both these figures had been regarded as guardians of the dead in the underworld.[45] So

there is an appropriateness to Hermes-Thoth appearing here. The parallel list in the *Gospel of the Egyptians* from Nag Hammadi has 'The second is Harmas, who is the eye of the fire...' and the missing line in our text may have said much the same thing.

3. Galila is probably a variation on the place name *Galilaea*, or Galilee, the location of much of Jesus' ministry in the New Testament Gospels.

4. Yobel is a Hebrew word meaning either 'trumpet' (specifically, the ram's horn), or the 'Jubilee', the fiftieth year, in which land was restored to its original family ownership and Israelite debt-slaves were freed.

5. Adonaios sounds like the Hebrew divine name *Adonai* with the Greek noun ending *os*. This is a good example of the kinds of names which Gnostic documents include. Often there is an unusual form of an already foreign name; this helps to create an impression of the exotic nature of the knowledge revealed to the Gnostic (especially in the case of names with Egyptian or Hebrew origins). It perhaps also conjures up a sense of antiquity, implying that the knowledge is truly ancient; this strategy was already practised by Jewish writers who attributed their works to primeval patriarchs like Enoch.

This is very much the impression created by the whole list, although our author probably did not come up with it himself. (It is closely paralleled in the *Gospel of the Egyptians* and in the *Apocryphon of John*.[46]) We have a mixture of linguistic elements from Hebrew and Greek, and of figures from the Old Testament as well as from Greek and Egyptian mythology, combining with the already complicated account of creation to form a compelling impression of esoteric *gnōsis*.

6. The Creation of Adam and Eve

Then Saklas said to his angels, 'Let us create a man according to the likeness and according to the image.' And they created Adam and his wife Eve, who in the cloud is called Zoë. For by this name (i.e. 'Adam'), all the generations inquire about him. But different generations call the woman by different names. And Sakla did not <53> command ... ... except (almost whole line missing) **generations** (almost whole line missing) this one (almost whole line missing).

And ... said to him, 'Your life is ... time, with your descendants.'

As in Genesis, the sequence of creations here closes with Adam and Eve coming on the scene. But the rationales behind the similar placings of Adam and Eve could hardly be more different. In Genesis, human beings are the climax of God's creative work, and are God's appointed stewards through whom he will govern creation. Here in the *Gospel of Judas*, however, the creative acts appear to have begun in heavenly purity, after which the only way is down. After the perfect cloud of light and the son Autogenes come the heavenly prototypes of Adamas and Seth who generate the entities which eventually result in the 'cosmos'; then the evil deities Nebro-Yaldabaoth and Saklas appear and create the gods of the underworld, with Saklas finally making Adam and Eve. So, far from humanity being the pinnacle of creation, in the Gnostic system the successively descending realities—further and further away from their source, the pure cloud of light—have eventually spluttered out Adam and Eve.

Again, Saklas takes on the character of the biblical God, with the language here deliberately picking up the creation account in Genesis: 'Then God said, "Let us make man in our image, in our likeness..."' (Gen. 1: 26). The image in which Saklas creates is probably that of Adamas, the heavenly prototype of Adam; in contrast to Adamas, however, Adam's lifespan has been limited. This limit has been presumably been set by Saklas, again playing the role of God in the Old Testament, who does the same (Gen. 6: 3).

This section also makes the point about Zoë being another name for Eve (Eve in Hebrew is related to the word for 'life', which is *zoē* in Greek). Although Adam's name is the same everywhere, people refer to Eve by two different names: some, perhaps Greek speakers, call her Zoë, others Eve. As we have seen, there is an interest in the *Gospel of Judas* in multiple names ('Cosmos' = 'Phthora'; 'Nebro' = 'Yaldabaoth') and the *Gospel of Philip* comments on Jesus' titles in different languages: 'The word "Christ" is "Messiah" in Syriac, but in Greek it is "Christ".'[47] The official language in the cloud is apparently Greek, as Eve is called Zoë there as well.

7. Concluding Dialogue on Creation

And Judas said to Jesus, 'What is the length of time (lit. 'amount') for which man will live?'

Jesus said to him, 'Why are you amazed that Adam with his generation received his allotted time where he received his allotted kingdom with his archon?'

Judas said to Jesus, 'Does the spirit of a man die?'

Jesus said, 'This is how God commanded Michael to loan the spirits of men to them so that they might serve. But the Great One commanded Gabriel to give the spirits—the spirits and the souls—to the great indomitable generation. For this reason, the rest of the souls <54> (almost two lines missing) light (almost two lines missing) to return ... ... spirit within you ... to dwell in this [flesh] in the generations of the angels. But God had them give knowledge to Adam and to those with him, so that the rulers of Chaos and Hades might not have dominion over them.'

The extensive monologue on creation is rounded off by a brief dialogue on the subject. Judas's first question does not receive a direct answer, but Jesus' answer does illuminate some of the *Gospel of Judas*'s understanding of creation. The first point is that Adam has an apportioned lifespan and dominion, and is accompanied in Eden by an archon.

In the discussion of the spirits, the archangel Michael apparently has the less appealing job of general spirit-dispensing, while Gabriel has the more privileged position of doling out the higher-grade spirits. The first class of people in the contrast is the lesser generations of men, deliberately put in their place by God, in a position of subordination ('so that they might serve'). The great generation, on the other hand (whose God is correspondingly called 'the Great One'), are the gentleman class—strangers to service, being indomitable, or, literally, 'kingless'.

This motif of 'kinglessness' is a common one in Gnostic literature, highlighting absolute elevation to the perfect divine fullness (the Gnostic 'Pleroma') above the dominating forces of the demiurge and other archons. It perhaps also connoted elevation above earthly rulers, and expressed something of the Gnostics' disaffection with the world in which they found themselves.[48]

Dialogue on the Hereafter (Continued)

4. The Destiny of the Cosmos

Judas said to Jesus, 'What, therefore, will become of those generations?'

Jesus said, 'Truly I say to you, when the stars over them all have completed their courses, and when Saklas has completed the times which have been appointed for him, their leading star will come with the generations, and the things which have been spoken of will be fulfilled. Then they will commit adultery in my name and they will kill their children <55> and (almost whole line missing) and (almost 8 lines missing) in my name and {and} your star will [rule] over the thirteenth aeon.' After that, Jesus laughed.

Judas said, 'Master, (almost one line missing).'

[Jesus] replied [and said], 'I am not laughing [at you], but at the error of the stars, because these six stars were deceived with these five warriors, and all these will perish with their creations.'

This section has two main themes, which are separated by the large gap in the middle. The first half is concerned with the events precipitated by history entering its final stage—there will apparently be an egregious outbreak of sin, perhaps perpetrated by the 'orthodox' Christians. (The sins are very much like those which the disciples see themselves committing in the Day 3 temple vision in Part I.) Then the period of Saklas's influence will come to an end.

In the second half, we have a reference to Judas's star presiding over the thirteenth aeon, which recalls the order of creation spelt out at the beginning: each aeon is served by a band of angels, but presided over by a luminary. The luminary in this case is Judas, or strictly speaking his star.

Thereafter, Jesus laughs, but the laughter is again far from being friendly heartiness. While Jesus is not laughing at Judas, he does seem to be amused by the fact that the stars and the mysterious 'warrior' figures have gone off course, and are going to be destroyed along with the entities they have brought into being. So Jesus in the *Gospel of Judas* has something of a wicked and merciless streak.

5. Judas's Destiny

Judas said to Jesus, 'What will become of those who have been baptized in your name?'

Jesus said, 'Truly, I say [to you], this baptism <56> (almost whole line missing) my name (almost one line missing) not (almost 8 lines missing) ... to me. Truly, [I] say to you, Judas, [those who] offer up sacrifice to Saklas ... god (almost 3 lines missing) everything which is evil. But you will be greater than them all. For you will sacrifice the man who carries me about. Already your horn has become exalted, your anger has burned, your star has passed overhead and your mind has [understood].'

The answer to Judas's question about the baptized has been lost here, but what does remain from this section has already attracted a lot of interest. There is a contrast between two parties here: the first is those who sacrifice to Saklas, the evil deity we have already seen is partner-in-crime with Nebro-Yaldabaoth; he also made Adam and Eve. The implication is almost certainly that he is the god of the disciples—this criticism of the Saklas-worshippers echoes the criticism of the disciples which we saw at the beginning of the text; we have also noted that Saklas is portrayed in the *Gospel of Judas* as the biblical creator God.

In contrast to those who offer service to Saklas, there is Judas. His sacrifice is infinitely greater than the offerings of the twelve disciples: he is to offer up to the chief priests the body of Jesus, the moveable platform for his real, transcendent being. Jesus is not necessarily instructing Judas to hand him over here, but merely prophesies it. Nevertheless, there is little doubt that this is pictured as a positive thing for Judas to accomplish: it will be the dramatic climax that he is to enact now that his 'horn is exalted' and his trial over, and afterwards the events of the end will come to pass. As such, Judas is perhaps a kind of true Gnostic priest here. The other disciples are pictured as murdering, adulterous priests who lead the masses astray (codex, pp. 38–40). In contrast, Judas is the ideal priest who acts, if not under Jesus' instructions, then at least in his service, presumably by releasing Jesus' spirit from its bodily imprisonment. Jesus is described here as not in essence a physical being, but rather as a spirit. A man 'carries him around': the original Greek word is used, for example, in Homer's *Iliad* in reference to the horses which bore Achilles (*Iliad*, 2.770).

<57> 'Truly [I say to you that] your (sing.) final [days] (almost two lines missing) become (almost three lines missing) grieve (almost two lines missing) the [archon] will be destroyed, [and] then the image of the great generation of Adam will be exalted, for that generation from the aeons exists before heaven and earth and the angels.

The end of this very fragmentary section is the only part which is at all clear. Adam's descendants are split into two groups, the hopeless generation which is lost, and the great generation which has spiritual kinship with Seth. This spiritual race will be exalted with its divine image at the end and be supreme, (presumably) taking the place of the governing 'archon' who will then be destroyed.

'Behold, everything has been told to you. Lift up your eyes and behold the cloud and the light which is in it, and the stars which surround it. The star which is the leader—that is your star.'

Previously, Judas was not complete. We saw earlier that Judas could not look Jesus in the eye (codex, p. 35), and that his star had deceived him (p. 45). Now, however, he has the *gnōsis*, the true revelation about the generation of the cosmos and of the generation of Adamas and Seth. His personal star is ahead of all the rest, whether the others here are the rest of the disciples in particular or the whole of the human race in general. The thinking here probably echoes Platonic thought as we have already seen, but perhaps also alludes to the Joseph story in the Old Testament. Joseph has two dreams about himself and his brothers, which he rather ill-advisedly recounts to them. This is the second: 'Behold, I have dreamed another dream, and behold the sun and the moon and eleven stars bowed down to me' (Gen. 37: 9).[49] The sun and the moon are Joseph's father and mother, and the eleven stars his brothers—like Judas, Joseph also has eleven companions who temporarily persecute him, but who will ultimately recognize his supremacy.

And Judas lifted up his eyes and saw the cloud of light and leapt into it. Those who stood underneath heard a voice coming from the cloud, which said: <58> (most of line missing) **great generation** (most of line missing) **image . . .** (most of line missing) **and . . .**

107

This scene recalls the transfiguration of Jesus in Matthew, Mark, and Luke in which Jesus ascends a high mountain with three of his disciples; a cloud of light overshadows them and the voice of God comes out from it.[50] What the cloud says is mostly lost here in the *Gospel of Judas*, but the cloud might very well be the same cloud of light which Jesus mentions at the very beginning of the creation mythology on page 47 of the codex. In mingling with this cloud, Judas has ascended to the highest level of knowledge and experience possible. Earlier (on page 45), Judas's star had deceived him into thinking he was ready to enter paradise ahead of his time, but now that he has attained to perfect *gnōsis* he is fully prepared. Despite the claims of some scholars, it seems extremely unlikely that this is a transfiguration of *Jesus*. The language points overwhelmingly towards Judas being the subject of the 'leaping'; he is the subject of the two prior verbs in the sequence. The assumption that only Jesus can be transfigured is simply based on the New Testament Gospels, and this—like many other ideas in the New Testament—may not hold for the *Gospel of Judas*. Certainly, in the next scene Judas is back in the earthly realm—as Jesus is after his transfiguration in the New Testament—but there is a big gap in the manuscript which would have given Judas ample opportunity to descend again.

Epilogue: The 'Betrayal'

(5 lines mostly missing) **Their chief priests were indignant that he had gone to his lodging place to pray. Some of the scribes were there looking out so that they might arrest him at prayer. For they feared the people, because they all held him as a prophet. And they advanced to Judas and they said to him,**

Translation and Interpretation

'Why are you here? You are the disciple of Jesus.' He answered them according to their wish. Judas took some money, and he handed [him] over to them.

The text, now lost, after the description of Judas's 'transfiguration' presumably described his subsequent return to the earthly sphere. Then come two slightly confusing sentences at the start of this section, after which the sequence of events is fairly easy to follow. In the canonical Gospels, Jesus has supper in a lodging room and then goes to the Garden of Gethsemane to pray. These two events are fused into one by the *Gospel of Judas* here, which makes it easier to understand why Judas is necessary to the chief priests and scribes—Jesus needs to be extricated from his lodging place. It is presumably this which Judas accomplishes for his fee.

Here endeth the lesson. Why the author stopped here is open to a number of interpretations. Was it just a case of everyone knowing the rest of the story? Perhaps, but even then the passion would probably only be omitted if it had been significantly downgraded in importance. And this may well be the case—it is after all only the anonymous human frame which is sacrificed, rather than the real spiritual essence of Jesus.

But the question of why the text ends here only arises if we are comparing the *Gospel of Judas* with the New Testament Gospels, which of course give the death of Jesus prime importance in their narratives. On its own terms, the *Gospel of Judas* actually has very little to do with Jesus *per se*, and everything to do with the heavenly knowledge he reveals: 'The secret message of the revelation which Jesus spoke to Judas Iscariot in the week leading up to the three days before he celebrated Passover.' Given this prologue, it is no surprise at all that the *Gospel of Judas* ends where it does: the work has fulfilled its goal of recounting the esoteric knowledge essential to Gnostic enlightenment, in forceful contrast to the alleged spiritual bankruptcy of the ecclesiastical establishment.

Title

The Gospel of Judas

At the beginning of the analysis of our text we categorized the *Gospel of Judas* as a 'Gnostic revelation dialogue', and we have seen several features of that genre: a question-and-answer format at a number of points, and secret revelation from Jesus. But the title at the end here (which is in the manuscript) gives further indication as to the nature of the work—it is a *Gospel*. This probably tells us that the general content of the work is the knowledge necessary for salvation, which we have already seen in any case: we see the tortuous progress of Judas from misguided, eucharist-celebrating disciple to trustee of the secrets of the Kingdom.

On the other hand, to call this work a 'Gospel' places it in a certain relation to other works called by the same name. By the time of the composition of *Judas*, this would certainly include the New Testament Gospels, Matthew, Mark, Luke, and John. But several others—such as the Gospels of Thomas and of Mary—may well pre-date the *Gospel of Judas* as well. On the basis of the attitude towards the disciples and established Christianity, it seems highly likely that the dismissal of the New Testament Gospels is implied. Despite this, Elaine Pagels has argued that the *Gospel of Judas* may have been intended to be read alongside them: 'Many regarded these secret Gospels not as radical alternatives to the New Testament Gospels, but as advanced-level teaching for those who had already received Jesus' basic message.'[51] But the central tenets of the *Gospel of Judas* are so opposed to those of Matthew, Mark, Luke, and John that this seems difficult to swallow: although we should not apply contemporary standards of consistency to ancient groups, we would have to assume someone reading the *Gospel of Judas* alongside the canonical Gospels to have an extremely high tolerance for contradiction.

On the other hand, this claim to secret revelation is probably not intended to undercut all other Gnostic Gospels (though it may have been opposed to some). The Gnostic creation mythology expounded by Jesus in Part II of the text here represents fairly mainstream Gnostic teaching, as can be seen by comparing the *Gospel of Judas* with the Nag Hammadi literature. At the same time, it is possible that this work was written for the specific needs of a particular group—a point which will be explored further in the next chapter.

By now, of course, we have become used to seeing Judas as something of a positive (though not only positive) figure in this work, but it is still striking to see the work entitled 'of Judas'. This is not necessarily a claim to *authorship*: the 'Book of Thomas the Contender' from Nag Hammadi, for example, is *revealed* to Thomas but written down by Mathaias. The point here is that the secret knowledge came through Judas.

What is the overall profile of this Judas in the work? Some have said that this closing title means not so much 'Good news according to . . .' in the conventional sense, but rather the 'Good news *about* Judas'.[52] According to the view promoted in the National Geographic publications, Judas is very much the 'most faithful friend and disciple'.[53] Bart Ehrman refers to Judas as the 'hero' of the Gospel.[54] On the other hand, there has been a reaction to this view, arguing that the *Gospel of Judas* still, or perhaps especially, has a negative view of the infamous disciple. One scholar, for example, has described the portrait in the *Gospel of Judas* as follows: 'Judas is guilty of sacrificing the man who wore Jesus, he is a demon, misled by his star, and he will never make it to the place reserved for the Holy Generation.'[55]

One of the difficulties here is that, as we have seen, some of the most important passages on this subject are highly contested. Is Judas promised that he certainly *will* ascend to the holy generation, or that he definitely will *not* (codex, pp. 46–7)? Who enters the cloud of light towards the end of the work? Is it Judas or Jesus (codex, p. 57)? These two passages are not completely clear as they stand, because of the gaps in the manuscript.

Certainly, within the work Judas is not a straightforwardly perfect figure. As a result of being misled by his star he gets things wrong (see e.g. p. 45), and asks silly questions (e.g. pp. 44, 53). But the disciples in the New Testament Gospels also make constant blunders, as is the case in apocryphal Gospels as well: Thomas makes a mistake in the *Gospel of Thomas* which earns him a correction from Jesus (*Thomas*, § 13), but there is no doubt that he is a positive figure.

In the *Gospel of Judas*, what is clear is that Judas is the recipient of special revelation, saving *gnōsis*. The closing title probably does not mean 'the good news about Judas', but it does underline the fact that this is the Gospel revealed to him: Judas receives what no human or angelic sense has previously perceived (codex, p. 47). It would be unlikely, if not impossible, for this revelation dialogue to be organized around a figure who is ultimately to be damned. On Day 1, he is undoubtedly pictured positively: he alone has the strength to stand before

Jesus, and makes the true confession about Jesus' origins. This concept of 'strength' is important: although the first mention of 'strong' is a reconstruction, later the disciples claim to be strong—even if only Judas is able to do what Jesus has asked. 'Strong' is an extremely positive term in the *Gospel of Judas*: the true chosen ones make up the 'strong and holy generation' (p. 36). On this same page in the codex Jesus describes Judas being replaced: 'For another will come to your place so that the twelve [disciples] might again be complete in their god' (p. 36). This is significant because Jesus thereby distinguishes himself and Judas on the one hand, from the remaining disciples' ('*their*') deluded worship on the other. In the penultimate episode in the work, before the 'betrayal', the transfiguration is almost certainly of *Judas*, not Jesus (p. 57).

So there is ambiguity around Judas in this work. He is not a figure of cloying piety, but nor is he likely to be an evil character whose destiny is destruction. There are certainly a number of confusing ambiguities in this Gospel. It seems, though, that he will join the holy generation, but only as a result of his understanding developing—in the course of his Gospel—from a mixture of insight and ignorance towards the perfect knowledge revealed by Jesus.

5

The Cainites

THE STARTLING transformation of Judas into a specially chosen disciple in his eponymous Gospel has provoked a flurry of
questions about the work. When was it written? Who produced
it? Was the author a lone religious maverick or did the work
represent the views of a group? Unfortunately, much of this
information has been lost in the mists of time. One reason for
this is that apart from the *Gospel of Judas* itself we have no
other texts which we can be sure come from the same group.
We have the writings of the Church Fathers, some of whom
provide snippets of information in connection with a book
they called 'the Gospel of Judas', but they to a man (they were
always men) condemn the work. So our evidence is only very
fragmentary. But history is made up of lots of fragments, so we
should examine them before giving up the quest altogether.

ST IRENAEUS AND THE *GOSPEL OF JUDAS*

The first author in antiquity to mention a Gospel of Judas is
Saint Irenaeus (*c*.130–*c*.200 CE). Irenaeus was Bishop of Lyon
in the latter part of the second century, and one of the first great

theologians of early Christianity. He has become rather notorious as a 'heresy hunter', as he is called in some of the recent *Gospel of Judas* literature, and was portrayed in the National Geographic documentary (complete with anachronistic writing desk) as a very serious, grumpy old man: Krosney labels him 'the enforcer from Gaul'.[1] But Irenaeus also writes with a dash of humour, even if it is mostly of the sarcastic variety, and directed against his enemies. He is at his best in mocking the obscurities and complexities of his Gnostic opponents:

For who would not spend everything they had in order to learn that the seas, springs, rivers and every liquid substance originate from the tears of the Enthymesis of the aeon which suffered...

I would very much like to contribute something myself to make this system blossom further. I have noticed that there are particular waters which are sweet—fountains, rivers, showers and the like. Others are salty, such as the sea, and so it is clear that these waters come from her tears, though I reckon that since she was formed with such agony and instability, she must have sweated a bit as well... But since there are also hot and pungent waters in the world—well, you can work out for yourself how she produces these, and from what part of her body she has discharged them. (*Against Heresies*, 1.4.3–4)

There exists a certain pre-beginning, royal, pre-unintelligible, pre-insubstantially powerful, and pre-whirled. Since it is a power, I call it 'Gourd'. With this Gourd there exists another power: I call it 'supervacuity'. Since this Gourd and this Supervacuity are one, they emitted, while not emitting, a fruit visible in its entirety, edible and sweet, which language calls 'Cucumber'. With this Cucumber there is a power of the same potency, which I call 'Melon'. These powers—Gourd, Supervacuity, Cucumber and Melon—emitted the remaining multitude of Valentinus' delirious Melons... (*Against Heresies*, 1.11.4)

The Cainites

On the other hand, Irenaeus also displays a real understanding of the recondite intricacies in the Gnostic systems which he discusses. His criticisms are certainly not merely superficial, but actually engage with the opposition on its own terms and often show an admirable grasp of the details, as we saw in the case of Judas and the twelfth aeon in Chapter 3.

Irenaeus and his Gospel of Judas

His most famous work (from which the excerpts above come) is *On the Detection and Refutation of Knowledge Falsely So Called*, more commonly known simply as *Against Heresies*. Irenaeus wrote the work in Greek, around 180 CE, but for the most part it only survives in a third- or fourth-century Latin translation. *Against Heresies* is an extensive defence of traditional Christian doctrine against as many of the threats to that doctrine that he could find, one of which is contained in a 'Gospel of Judas':

Others again say that Cain came from a higher Power, and claim that Esau, Korah and the Sodomites and all such people are their ancestors. They also claim that because of this, they have been attacked by the creator, but that none of them has actually been harmed. For Lady Wisdom ('Sophia') snatched away from them what belonged to her. They say that Judas the betrayer knew these things very well, and that he alone—more than the other disciples—knew the truth and so accomplished the mystery of the betrayal. So they say that through him all things, both earthly and heavenly, were dissolved. And they put forward a fabricated book to this effect, which they call the 'Gospel of Judas'. But I have also made a collection of their writings in which they advocate the destruction of the works of Hystera ('womb'). (*Against Heresies*, 1.31.1–2)

The Cainites

In some editions of the *Against Heresies* this section is prefaced with the heading 'On the Cainites', and this has misled some scholars into thinking that Irenaeus wrote the heading himself and knew about a group of this name. In one of the National Geographic publications, Bart Ehrman writes: 'One of the many Gnostic groups that Irenaeus discussed was called the Cainites. We don't know if this group really existed or if Irenaeus simply made their name up—there is no independent record of their existence.'[2] Ehrman is questioning Irenaeus's trustworthiness here but, ironically, it is Ehrman who has made a mistake.

Irenaeus scholars have in fact regarded these 'chapter headings' (in Latin *capitula* or *argumenta*) as later additions. The two scholars who have produced the definitive, magisterial ten-volume edition of Irenaeus' *Against Heresies* comment that it 'seems certain' that the headings do not go back to Irenaeus in the second century. The early twentieth-century Cambridge don and Church of England cleric J. Armitage Robinson comments that the headings are 'quite futile', often 'breaking the sense and causing unnecessary difficulties in interpretation'. Another comments: 'There is no reason, as far as we are concerned, to encumber the text of Irenaeus with these titles, which are basically "foreign bodies"'. In fact, there was a two-stage process which produced them.[3]

First of all, some time after Irenaeus there is 'the person who drew up the table of contents', which was probably written in Greek, and put at the beginning of the *Against Heresies*. Then, secondly, after the *Against Heresies* had been translated into Latin, a scribe inserted these headings at the beginnings of the relevant (or, sometimes, irrelevant) sections. As the modern editors of the *Against Heresies* note: 'The result is pitiful, because to the disorder of the table of contents the "rubricator" has added the incoherence of how they are placed.'[4]

So no Cainites in Irenaeus. Scholars may want, for convenience, to refer to the group described by Irenaeus under this name, but it needs to be remembered, lest one fall into the same trap as Ehrman, that the first evidence that we have for the name post-dates Irenaeus.[5]

In any case, this work apparently does see Cain (the first-born son of Adam and Eve) as well as Esau, Korah, and the Sodomites as the group's spiritual ancestors. These figures are all notoriously bad characters from the Old Testament, some of whom had already been connected in early Jewish and Christian tradition: the Epistle of Jude (in fact, another 'Judas') in the New Testament links Cain and Korah and, as we have seen, the *Acts of Thomas* has Cain, Esau, and Judas next to one another in a list of people who are examples of immorality. So the Gnostics who are behind the work mentioned by Irenaeus are obviously attempting to turn the tables on the Bible and claim that the possessors of true knowledge are actually those whom the Bible paints as the villains. On the other hand, the God who created the world and punished these characters is, for Irenaeus's opponents here, actually the true villain of the piece.

The position Irenaeus is describing is a Gnostic one: this group claimed *gnōsis*, or true knowledge, to the effect that the creator was actually a much lesser deity than the true Father who is at the very top of the heavenly realms, above all the other divinities. According to our Irenaeus quotation, one of the higher deities whom this group claimed to have on its side is Lady Wisdom, or Sophia. She, apparently, snatched away the souls of these rehabilitated Old Testament villains so that when the creator attacked them he would only harm their bodies and so not do any real damage. Thereafter, Irenaeus mentions the 'Gospel of Judas', describing it as a 'fabricated book' and perhaps implying that he thinks this group wrote it: he clearly does not entertain the idea that it came from Judas himself.

It is difficult to know how carefully Irenaeus had read the work, if at all. In the final sentence of the extract above, he may be contrasting the fact that he has collected the 'Hystera' books with the absence of the Gospel of Judas from his library.[6] Or he may simply be drawing a distinction between the contents of the Gospel of Judas and the even stranger 'womb' literature. In any case, as others have already mentioned, he would not need to read it: the very title of the book would mark it out for Irenaeus as heretical.[7]

This subsequent reference to writings about the abolition of the works of Hystera might point to a family connection between this Gospel of Judas and the Greek Gospel of the Egyptians, which also comes from the second century CE. In it, there is a saying attributed to Jesus: 'I have come to destroy the works of the female', the connection being that Irenaeus has mentioned 'destroying the works of the womb (*Hystera*)'. So this group perhaps influences or is influenced by the Gospel of the Egyptians, or at any rate has links with it. We will see a connection with another second-century Gospel shortly.

Are they the Same Gospel of Judas?

The big question, however, is whether there is a link between Irenaeus and the Coptic text we now have. If our *Gospel of Judas* and that of Irenaeus are one and the same, then we would be able to make some headway with questions about the date of the work and about the kind of people who made use of it. In the excitement that has surrounded the *Gospel of Judas* in recent times, many have jumped to the conclusion that our text simply must be the one talked about by Irenaeus of Lyon. Krosney's *The Lost Gospel* assumes they are one and the same, and this is also apparent in James Robinson's *Secrets of Judas*:[8] 'In the middle of the second century, a *Gospel of Judas* was written by a Gnostic sect called Cainites. Of course it was promptly suppressed, but apparently it is this same document that has been rediscovered in our own time.' This may 'apparently' be the case for Robinson, but it is not something that can simply be assumed, especially when Robinson had not even seen the Coptic *Gospel of Judas* when he wrote his book.

Gregor Wurst, Professor of Church History at the University of Augsburg, has set out the arguments in support of the connection. He comments that two points are prominent in Irenaeus' account of this group: first, that Judas has the special knowledge about Jesus as no other disciple does, and—second—that the betrayal is seen as contributing to the 'dissolution of all earthly and heavenly things'. Wurst then makes the link: 'These two thoughts run throughout the new Coptic Gospel of Judas.'[9]

This sounds very reasonable. But, on the other side, there are also reasons which might cast some doubt. First, it is true that the theme of Judas's special knowledge is a feature of both works—but this is a theme which we would expect of any ancient document called 'The Gospel of Judas': in the *Gospel of Thomas*, Thomas knows the truth better than the other disciples; in the *Gospel of Mary*, Mary receives a revelation privately from Jesus, and so on. So to say that two references to a Gospel of Judas must be talking about the same work on the basis of this is a little hazardous.

The second point in common mentioned by Wurst is that the betrayal according to Irenaeus seems somehow to be a trigger for the 'dissolution of all earthly and heavenly things'. Wurst admits here that 'our Coptic text is unfortunately not as clear', which is inevitable because of the damage to the manuscript on the final pages.[10] He speculates about what is 'destroyed' in a reference to destruction on page 55 of the manuscript which talks about the wandering stars, the five combatants, and their creatures—hence the 'heavenly' (the stars and the combatants, or warriors) and the 'earthly things' (their creations).[11] However, again we should remain cautious here.

While we would certainly want to allow for some imprecision in the process of Irenaeus's own conceptualizing of his *Gospel of Judas* (especially if he had not even read it), it is by no means clear that the 'creations' of the stars and the warriors belong to the 'earthly things': we have seen that there is a complicated sequence of creations by a vast number of heavenly figures, the result often being more divine, angelic figures—a point of which Irenaeus is well aware.

On the other hand, it is probably difficult to make too much of this phrase in either direction, because Irenaeus's language closely resembles a statement in the *Gospel of Mary*:

So, through him all things—both earthly and heavenly—were dissolved. (Irenaeus)

But I have recognized that the all is being dissolved, both the earthly things and the heavenly. (*Gospel of Mary*, 15, 21–2)

As a result, Irenaeus is probably making use of a Gnostic formula here, rather than summarizing the work in his (or the Gospel of Judas's) own words.

In consequence of all this, there is still need for a bit more circumspection in the whole matter. This might sound rather pernickety and over-cautious, but the problem is that we often come across quotations in the Church Fathers from named Gnostic works, but then when we look in the works we have under those names the quotations are not there. For example, the early Christian writer Hippolytus's 'quotation' from what he calls the *Gospel of Thomas* starts with a couple of motifs which might come from different parts of our *Thomas*, but then goes off into unknown territory. Similarly, Epiphanius (a writer we are about to explore) refers to a work which he calls the *Gospel of Philip*, but the passage which he quotes does not match up with what we know as the *Gospel of Philip*. Again, the fourth-century Church Father Jerome talks about a quotation by the Apostle Paul (in 1 Cor. 2: 9) from the *Apocalypse of Elijah* but which has no resemblance to any of the texts of this Elijah book which have survived.

One reason for this may be that we know of a number of cases in which different Gospels or Gnostic works in antiquity had the same name. There are, for example, at least two different works which go by the title 'the Gospel of the Egyptians' (we have already mentioned one), and two works—copied one after the other in the same manuscript—named 'the Apocalypse of James'. Similarly then, there may, confusingly, be at least two Gospels of Judas.[12]

Finally, if they do turn out to be one and the same work, it is at least surprising that there is no mention in the newly discovered *Gospel of Judas* of Cain or any of the other rehabilitated

Old Testament villains mentioned in Irenaeus's account. The problem of Cain being absent is perhaps exacerbated further by the prominence of 'Adamas' and 'Seth' in our text. Although these figures are heavenly archetypes rather than the people of the biblical book of Genesis, the mythology of these divine prototypes is based on the fact that, in Genesis, Adam's first two sons are removed from the picture. Abel is killed and Cain is doomed to be a wanderer on the earth, and goes off to Nod (Gen. 4: 8, 12). Seth is a new beginning, a new son of Adam, and for Eve a son in the place of Abel (Gen. 4: 25). So the Gnostic Seth mythology works precisely by jumping straight from Adam to Seth and devaluing, rather than beatifying, Cain.

The upshot is that we must at least wonder whether the widespread assumption that these two Gospels of Judas are one and the same is correct. It *may* be: the lack of close correlation between Irenaeus and our Coptic text could be because Irenaeus has not actually read the work. Alternatively, there may have been different editions floating about: Lyon is a decent-ish distance from Egypt, and so it may have undergone some changes on the journey; similarly, some of the features which Irenaeus notes might have been lost in translation when the work was put into Coptic. So there is, after all, a sporting chance that Irenaeus is referring to what is to all intents and purposes our *Gospel of Judas*.

OTHER REFERENCES TO THE 'CAINITES'

Shortly after Irenaeus, the group which made use of Irenaeus's 'Gospel of Judas' had certainly been given the name 'Cainites' or 'Cainists' (*Cainaei* in Latin, *Kainistai* in Greek). The first writer we know to have used the name is Clement of Alexandria, who wrote seven books of 'Patchwork Miscellanies' (which live up to their name in their lack of apparent organization and purpose) sometime between 193 and his death around 214–215 CE. In the final book of these 'Stromateis' he discusses the way in which some heresies are named after their founders, such figures as Valentinus, Marcion, and Basilides; others derive their names from their place of origin, others from their beliefs or practices. Towards the end, 'others derive their names from the persons to whom they give honour, like the Cainites and those called the Ophites' (*Stromateis*, VII. xvii. § 17). Clement's reference does not give much away about these Cainites, however.

Around the same time, they are rather more significant for the lawyer and theologian Tertullian. He mentions the Cainites in an aside in his *Prescription against Heretics* (*c*.200 CE); here they are apparently reviving an immoral heresy from New Testament times (*Prescription*, 33). But he also wrote an entire work, *On Baptism* (also *c*.200 CE), because 'a certain viperess of the Cainite heresy, who was recently active here, has snatched away a great number with her most poisonous doctrine, above all in her attempt to destroy baptism' (*On Baptism*, 1). This was probably in Carthage in North Africa. In the course of the next generation or so there are references to them again in Hippolytus (*Refutation of All Heresies*, 8; *c*.225 CE) and Origen (*Against Celsus*, 3.13; *c*.250 CE). But these statements do not add to our knowledge of the group.

A work falsely attributed to Tertullian called *Against All Heresies* (by now the genre is well established) is slightly later but probably still from the third century CE. It gives a great deal of information about the Cainites and alleges that there were two versions of the group's doctrine, both of which go into more detail about Judas's actions than does Irenaeus:

Yet another heresy has broken out, called that of the 'Cainites'...For some of them think that one should be grateful to Judas for this reason [sc. because of the benefits he has brought to the world]. For, they say, Judas noticed that Christ wanted to subvert the truth, and so betrayed him so that that truth could not be subverted.

But others disagree and say the opposite. Rather, since the Powers of this world did not want Christ to suffer, lest through his death salvation might be obtained for the human race, he (Judas) took thought for this salvation of the human race and betrayed Christ. As a result, the salvation which was being impeded by the Powers who stood in the way of Christ suffering could not be impeded in any way, and therefore the salvation of the human race through the passion of Christ could not be delayed. (*Against All Heresies*, II.5–6)

Both of these views, rather clumsily expressed by our unknown author, are peculiar. In the first, Jesus is the villain—this is clearly not an idea on the radar screen of the author of our *Gospel of Judas*. In the second version of events, Jesus is scarcely an actor in the drama at all: although he is the means of salvation, the real battle goes on between Judas and the Powers. This is a rather better fit with our text.

A century later again, an account turns up in the *Book of Diverse Heresies*, by Philastrius, Bishop of Brescia in Northern Italy. In this book, which he probably wrote some time between 383 and 391 CE, the group who founded their heresy on Judas follow the second of the two options above, and regard Judas as the mediator of heavenly *gnōsis*:

The Cainites

Others again founded a heresy from Judas the traitor, saying that he performed a good work because he betrayed the saviour. For he, it [*i.e.* the heresy] states, appeared to us as the author of all good knowledge, through whom the heavenly mysteries are revealed to us. (*Book of Diverse Heresies*, XXXIV.1)

Again, Philastrius, like Pseudo-Tertullian, does not actually mention a work called 'the Gospel of Judas', even though his summary of Cainite doctrine here—while very brief—is close to what we have in our text.

EPIPHANIUS

A Gospel of Judas is mentioned again by a contemporary of Philastrius, Epiphanius of Salamis (*c*.315–403 CE), who in the 370s wrote a book engagingly entitled *Medicine Chest against the Heresies*. In fact, according to one of the leading experts on the work, Epiphanius wrote the enormous *Panarion* (the Greek word for 'medicine chest') in less than three years.[13] Epiphanius not only mentions a Gospel of Judas, but does so explicitly in connection with the Cainites, the thirty-eighth sect (out of eighty!) which he discusses, just prior to the 'Sethians':

Again, another sect is the 'Sethians', as they are called. It is not found everywhere, nor is the sect called 'the Cainites' before it. Perhaps most of these too have already been uprooted. For what is not from God cannot stand. It grows for a time, but cannot properly survive. I think perhaps I came across this sect in Egypt. (I cannot exactly remember where I came across them.) And some things I discovered about it by personal investigation as an eyewitness, the rest I learned about it from other books. (*Panarion*, 39, 1.1–2)

From this, then, Epiphanius seems to imply that there are pockets of resistance in which Sethians and Cainites continue to survive, albeit in very small numbers. But his statements are rather vague, and so do not amount to much.

One of Epiphanius's principal sources is Irenaeus, which means that the picture of Judas and his Gospel which he supplies is quite a familiar one:

And because of this they say that Judas knew all about them (Esau, Cain, *et al.*). For the Cainites want to have him as their ancestor too, and count him exceedingly knowledgeable, such that they use a short work named after him, which they call 'The Gospel of Judas'. (*Panarion*, 38, 1.5)

So Judas, one of the spiritual ancestors of the Cainites, writes his Gospel (a 'short' work—but how short?) because of his supreme enlightenment. In fact, in its 'summary' of the Cainites, the *Panarion* says that they actually deify Judas, but these summaries—like the chapter headings in Irenaeus—are probably by a later author.[14]

In addition to information which we already know from earlier writers, Epiphanius reports that the Gospel of Judas and the group's writings about Womb are not their only faked documents. These Cainites are apparently compulsive forgers:

Again, another book has come to my attention in which they have forged certain statements full of lawlessness, and it contains such remarks as, 'This is the angel who blinded Moses, and these are the angels who hid the companions of Korah, Dathan and Abiram, and took them away.' Again, others forge another short work named after the Apostle Paul, full of disgrace. (The so-called Gnostics also use it.) They call it 'The Ascension of Paul', following the apostle's statement that he has ascended to the third heaven and heard unutterable words, which no-one can say. And these, they say, are the unutterable words. (*Panarion*, 38, 2.4–5)

Epiphanius also makes reference not only to the group's strange taste in literature and theological unorthodoxy, but also to the rather dubious moral universe which they inhabit. Though his account is similar to that of Irenaeus, Epiphanius's version is perhaps the more well preserved and eloquent:

And they say, as Carpocrates does, that no-one can be saved unless they go through all things. For each of them, using this excuse, does unspeakable things and acts disgracefully, and commits all the sins they can, while calling on the name of each angel (both real angels, and their own which they have invented). And to each of these angels he attaches a certain lawless deed from amongst earthly sins, by offering up his own action in the name of whichever angel he wishes. And whenever they do these things, they say as follows: 'O Angel So-and-so, I carry out your work. O Authority So-and-so, I do your deed'. And this is perfect knowledge to them, since the excuses for their lawless disgrace brazenly derive—yes!—from the aforementioned mothers and fathers of the sects. I am referring to the Gnostics and Nicolaus, as well as to Valentinus and Carpocrates, their associates. (*Panarion*, 38, 1.6–2.3)

What we appear to have in this report is a kind of ritualized immorality, allegedly tied to the Cainites' cosmology, in which the angels and powers somehow preside over what the 'worshippers' are doing. The Cainites, then, reputedly practised rituals which involved deliberately breaking biblical laws, and breaking them so comprehensively that they would attain to a complete, immoral perfection in order to be saved. The main idea here is again that the Cainites claimed to have secret knowledge of a truth which is almost a mirror-image of what is in the

Bible: in addition to the villains of the Bible being their heroes and vice versa, what is depicted as immorality in the Bible is actually a kind of worship to them. So, according to Epiphanius, the Gospel of Judas which he mentions appears to have kept some strange company.

But scholars are often particularly suspicious of accounts by the champions of orthodoxy when they go in for accusations of immorality among Gnostic groups. Often the heresiologists did not have first-hand knowledge of movements they were writing about, as per Epiphanius's statement above about his information on the Sethian sect: 'I discovered some things about it in an actual encounter, by inquiry, but have learned others from the literature.' As a result, he, along with other orthodox writers, may have seen moral corruption as simply part and parcel of having strange beliefs.

On Epiphanius's side, perhaps, is the Cainites' rather strange collection of patron saints: Cain murdered his brother; Esau then tried to murder Jacob; Korah was a rebel; the Sodomites were proverbial for their immorality. The complicated relation between the ritual activity and the angels might also speak in favour of it being a Gnostic idea rather than simply a product of anti-heretical gossip. Ultimately, we cannot really know whether there is any truth in these reports, and we have in any case already seen that the Coptic *Gospel of Judas* is not written by someone this way inclined. Its author in fact turns the tables on the orthodox: as he says in one of the passages about the last days, 'they will commit adultery in my name and they will kill their children' (codex, p. 54). So, on this point, Epiphanius is almost certainly not helping with the profile of our author, whether because he is inaccurate about their practices, or because he is talking about a different Gospel of Judas.

THEODORET

Finally, we have another discussion of the Cainites and their Gospel of Judas from the fifth-century Bishop of Cyr, Theodoret (*c*.393–*c*.466 CE). In his *Compendium of Heretical Fables* many of the same ideas are trotted out again. Cain and his descendants are hated by the creator God, but protected by Sophia; for these Cainites, Judas alone of all the disciples knew the real truth. But Theodoret supplements this with an explanation of why he thinks the *Gospel of Judas* cannot be genuine: 'They even cite a Gospel as written by him, which they themselves composed. For he soon put on the noose— the punishment for his betrayal' (*Compendium*, I.15). In other words, Theodoret does not consider it to have been historically possible for Judas to have composed a Gospel account of his own: after all, immediately after betraying Jesus, Judas hanged himself. There would not be time, Theodoret reasons, for Judas to have written his memoirs.

ASSESSMENT

So the questions about who wrote the *Gospel of Judas*, when, and why have at least some answers. It is, first off, quite likely that Irenaeus is talking about a group which went on to be named 'the Cainites', even if he does not actually mention the name himself.[15] Secondly, it is plausible, though by no means as certain as some have maintained, that he is talking about a work which is substantially the same as our *Gospel of Judas*, though almost certainly in his time in its original Greek form.

If this is the case, then it follows that our *Gospel of Judas* dates back to the period before 180 CE, and that it may have been produced by the Cainites. It is possible that there may also have been different editions of the work: this could account for some of the differences between our copy and the ideas mentioned by Irenaeus. Finally, it has to be said that it is unlikely that these Cainites were Gnostic libertines, and especially unlikely that the author of our *Gospel of Judas* was that way inclined. So we have some fragments of information about our newly discovered text, even if it still retains a good deal of mystery.

6

Rewriting History

EVEN IF we do not know everything we might like to about the *Gospel of Judas*, we are by no means completely in the dark. In its Coptic incarnation as we have it, the work found its final resting place in Middle Egypt, perhaps as the property of a single individual. But, beyond that, we do not have many other leads. It is almost certain that, like the vast majority of Gnostic works surviving in Coptic, it was originally written in Greek. However, Stephen Emmel has bemoaned the lack of evidence that we have from antiquity about the translators of Greek texts into Coptic.[1] As far as the *Gospel of Judas*'s Greek career is concerned, we saw in the previous chapter that there is at least a sporting chance that the 'Gospel of Judas' mentioned by Irenaeus is the same as ours, and so it may well have been the Cainites who made use of it.

But can we go back any further, and glean anything more about when it was originally written? More importantly, could there be anything in the conclusion Herb Krosney draws about these Cainites? 'If an entire sect believed that the great betrayal had in fact been ordered by Jesus and carried out by his favoured disciple, that interpretation could, after study, become as valid as the version told in the New Testament.'[2] Does the *Gospel of Judas*, then, have the potential to overthrow our traditional understandings of Judas and Jesus?

DATING THE *GOSPEL OF JUDAS*

Taking Codex Tchacos as our starting point, we have already noted in Chapter 1 that carbon dating has shown the manuscript to have come from the third or fourth century CE, specifically 280 CE, ±60 years. So the dating of the manuscript provides us with a 'terminus ante quem', that is, a latest possible date for the *Gospel of Judas*'s composition. The date of around 280 CE is too late, however, because the original is certainly older than our Coptic translation. So we need to go back earlier than 280 CE to allow time for the work to gain sufficient kudos to warrant being translated from its Greek original.

So if some time around the mid-third century gives us a *latest* possible point in time for the composition of the original *Gospel of Judas*, what is the earliest? The last historical event described in it—Judas handing Jesus over—obviously means that the *Gospel of Judas* must have been written after the early 30s CE. But does the work display influence from any of the later literary records of the activities of Jesus and Judas?

Some have judged that the reference to Judas being replaced by another disciple after his death means that the *Gospel of Judas* certainly knew the account of this in the book of Acts.[3] But it is possible that the author merely knew the traditional version of events in which Matthias took Judas's place. Probably clearer, on the other hand, are the indications that the *Gospel of Judas* is dependent upon the New Testament Gospels for some of its phraseology, and most of the evidence for this comes at the very beginning and the very end of our Coptic text, the places where there is some overlap with the traditional story. One significant influence on the *Gospel of Judas*, as we will see, is the Gospel of Matthew.

The Influence of the Gospel of Matthew

Very near the end of the *Gospel of Judas*, the strongest evidence of influence comes in the two sentences about Jesus' opponents wanting to capture him but being too afraid: these statements are very closely paralleled in Matthew. Not only do Matthew and the *Gospel of Judas* have much in common in the way they describe this incident, but the *Gospel of Judas* also reproduces some of the ways in which Matthew has modified his source, the version in Mark.

Mark 12: 12	Matt. 21: 46	*Gospel of Judas*, p. 58
(i) And	And	Some of the scribes
(ii) they were seeking to arrest him,	seeking to arrest him,	were there looking out so that they might arrest him in the house of prayer.
(iii) but they feared the crowd	they feared the crowds,	For they feared the people,
(iv)	because they held him (some MSS: 'as') a prophet	because they all held him as a prophet.

It is generally accepted by scholars that Mark was written first, and was also a source for Matthew's Gospel. What these parallel columns above show, then, is a gradual development from

Mark, to Matthew, to the *Gospel of Judas.* In sections (i) and (ii) Matthew sticks very closely to Mark's original version, and the *Gospel of Judas* adapts the language, without changing much of the sense. In (iii) Mark has 'crowd', which becomes in Matthew 'crowds', plural, and finally something different—'the people'— in *Judas.* Finally, and most importantly, Matthew's last clause ('because they held...') is a late addition into the way the story is told, and this later explanation from Matthew then finds its way into our Coptic Gospel. By far the best explanation for these differences—the last in particular—is that Mark influenced Matthew, then Matthew influenced the *Gospel of Judas.*

A number of minor indications also point to the *Gospel of Judas*'s indebtedness to Matthew. On the first page, one very small point is the spelling of Judas's second name, 'Iscariot'. In Mark, the name is consistently spelled *Iskarioth*, whereas in Matthew and John the spelling is *Iskariotēs*, which is what we have in the *Gospel of Judas* (p. 33 [restored], p. 35).[4] On the other hand, Matthew and Mark have in common the plot against Jesus coming together two days before Passover; this fits with the prologue to the *Gospel of Judas* in which the revelations of Jesus to Judas take place in the week running up to the *third* day before. (This, as we saw in Chapter 4, could mean two days before in the conventional English sense, or it could be that the day after Judas has been told of his mission he then fulfils it.) Additionally, the idiom for celebrating the Passover here (literally, 'doing Passover') is most closely paralleled in the New Testament Gospels in Matthew 26: 18.[5] Another possible indication, still on the first page, comes in the summary of Jesus' public ministry; here the author refers to 'some walking in the way of righteousness', which perhaps draws on Matthew's reference to the 'way of righteousness'—he is the only evangelist and New Testament author to use the phrase (Matt. 21: 32).

In the central sections of the *Gospel of Judas*, there are only some small points of overlap. To take one example:

Truly, I say to you, no one has arisen, among those born of women, greater than John the Baptist. But the one who is least in the kingdom of heaven is greater than he. (Matt. 11: 11)

Truly [I] say to you, [no-]one born [of] this aeon will see that [generation]. No army of star-angels will rule over that generation. Nor will anyone born of mortal man be able to accompany it. (*Gospel of Judas*, p. 37)

Although the subject matter here is different, we have a stylistic similarity, in which two stock phrases occur together: the introductory 'Truly, I say to you . . .' formula, combined with the 'no one born of . . .' motif. On a similar note, Matthew alone among the evangelists follows up the 'Truly, I say to you . . .' formula with another: 'Again I say to you . . .':

Truly, I say to you, whatever you bind on earth will be bound in heaven, and whatever you loose on earth shall be loosed in heaven.
Again I say to you, if two of you agree on earth about anything you request, it will be done for you by my Father in heaven. (Matt. 18: 18–19)

Truly, I say to you, only with difficulty will a rich person enter the kingdom of heaven.
Again I say to you, it is easier for a camel to pass through the eye of a needle than for a rich person to enter the kingdom of God. (Matt. 19: 23–4)

Truly, I say to you, all the priests who were standing at that altar call upon my name.

Again I say to you, my name has been written on [this house] for the generations of stars by the generations of men. (*Gospel of Judas*, p. 39)

So, again, a distinctive feature of Matthew's material has crept into the *Gospel of Judas*.

The last two pages have a few more indications. In the 'transfiguration' of Judas near the end of the document, Judas enters a 'cloud of light' (codex, p. 57). It is noticeable that of the three roughly parallel accounts in Matthew, Mark, and Luke in the New Testament, Matthew is the only one to mention that the cloud at Jesus' transfiguration is a 'luminous cloud', or, in a few manuscripts, a 'cloud of light' (Matt. 17: 5).

What survives of the last page begins with: 'And their chief priests were indignant…' (codex, p. 58). The only parallel to this in the New Testament Gospels is again in Matthew: 'But when the chief priests and the scribes saw the wonderful things that he did, and the children crying out in the temple, "Hosanna to the Son of David!" they were indignant…' (Matt. 21: 15).

Finally, the question which the scribes ask Judas in the last few lines of the *Gospel of Judas* is very similar to one interpretation of the cryptic question (or command) of Jesus in Matthew 26:

Jesus said to him, '*Friend, why are you here?*' (*Or:* 'Friend, do what you came to do.') Then they came up and took Jesus and arrested him. (Matt. 26: 50)

And they advanced to Judas and they said to him, '*Why are you here? You are the disciple of Jesus.*' (*Gospel of Judas*, p. 58)

Most of these examples are only small indications, and some may be mere coincidence.[6] But, since there are a good number of them, when taken together they do suggest the influence of the Gospel of Matthew. Particularly illuminating is Matthew's editorial note about the anxiety of the Jewish leaders finding its way into the *Gospel of Judas*.

To many scholars, this will hardly be surprising. In 1950, Édouard Massaux concluded his monumental study of the influence of Matthew: 'Until the end of the second century, the first gospel remained the gospel par excellence. People looked to Mt. for the teaching which conditioned Christian behavior, so that the Gospel of Mt. became the norm for Christian life.'[7] More recently, Christopher Tuckett has noted the same tendency in the Gnostic literature from Nag Hammadi: 'Of all the synoptic allusions noted here, by far the greatest number show affinities with Matthew's Gospel.'[8]

But this is by no means to suggest that the author of the *Gospel of Judas* sat pen in hand with a copy of Matthew's Gospel in front of him. The point is rather that the popularity of Matthew in the second century and beyond meant that most writers would have heard (or, in a minority of cases, read) the Gospel stories in their Matthean forms. So they would have most readily reproduced them in a way which reflected Matthew's phraseology.

Most scholars date Matthew's Gospel to around 80 CE. So, at the opposite end from our latest possible date (sometime before 280 CE), we have *c*.80 CE as a *terminus a quo*. But then we have to account for the fact that 80 CE is too early for the *Gospel of Judas*, since we would need to allow time for Matthew's Gospel to circulate and begin to have an importance sufficient for it to begin influencing other works. There are still other factors which make a date before 100 CE virtually impossible.

Rewriting History

The Portrayal of the 'Church' in the Gospel of Judas

The vision of the temple on pages 38–40 of the manuscript also offers some important clues as to when the *Gospel of Judas* was written. This is because of the kind of Church structure and practice which is presupposed there: in this vision 'priests' are conducting the service and 'sacrificing' at the 'altar'. Although the Church in the New Testament period was not without its officials (overseers, deacons, etc.), the picture in this temple vision does seem to represent a later, post-New Testament development. In fact, Christian leaders were not called priests until a considerable time later, but the Apostolic Fathers at the end of the first and into the second century did think in terms of the eucharist being a sacrifice at an altar:

For it will not be a small sin if we cast aside from the episcopacy those who have 'offered the gifts' blamelessly and in holiness (1 Clement 44.4: *c*.95–96 CE)

Therefore, be eager to take part in the one eucharist. For there is one flesh of our Lord Jesus Christ, and one cup for the oneness of his blood. There is one altar, just as there is one bishop ... (Ignatius, *Letter to the Philadelphians*, 4: *c*.114 CE)

On the Lord's Day, when you gather together, break bread and give thanks, confessing your sins so that your sacrifice will be pure ... (*Didache*, 14: *c*.110 CE)

This means that this episode in the *Gospel of Judas* is very unlikely to go back to Jesus and the disciples: these first references to eucharistic sacrifice in the Apostolic Fathers represent the beginning of a theological tendency which is seen in fairly full bloom in the *Gospel of Judas's* temple vision, where we have all the components in place: priests, temple, altar, and sacrifices. Hence, rather than going back to the first century, it is much more likely to be part of our author's polemic against the emerging Church establishment in the second.

Gnostic Features in the Gospel of Judas

The theological ideas in the *Gospel of Judas*, as almost all scholars involved in the discussion so far have noted, place it in the second century at the earliest. The 'aeon of Barbelo', and characters such as 'Autogenes', 'Saklas', and 'Yaldabaoth' all crop up for the first time in the second century—in Irenaeus and the Gnostic literature that probably dates back to that period. The names 'Adamas' (related to 'Adam', but also derived, according to Irenaeus, from the Greek word for 'unconquerable') and 'Zoë' (Greek for 'life') point to a Greek-speaking environment, whereas Jesus almost certainly taught in Aramaic. And the heavy influence of Plato (his idea of individuals having companion-stars, for example) on the creation mythology in the revelation to Judas points to a Greek-*thinking* author.

As a result of all these factors, some time between 140 and 220 CE is a reasonable estimate of when the original Greek text of the *Gospel of Judas* was composed and in the first half of this eighty-year span if our *Gospel of Judas* is the same as that of Irenaeus.

Additions in the Coptic Version?

A final factor which complicates the historical picture further is the presence of a possible Coptic pun in our text. Judas's confession of Jesus, in which he acknowledges Jesus as having come from the aeon of Barbelo, ends with the statement that 'the one who sent (*taouo*) you is the one whose name I am not worthy to speak (*taouo*)' (codex, p. 35). This is apparently a play on the two meanings of this same verb *taouo*. As we have said, it is highly likely that the *Gospel of Judas* as we have it was translated into Coptic from Greek, but the pun here would almost certainly not go back to a Greek original since neither of the most common words for 'send' in Greek can also mean 'say' (or vice versa). So probably this is the result of later additions to the Coptic version of the work: it is much less likely that the translator would incorporate a pun in the normal course of translation, meaning that this sentence and perhaps some of the surrounding context as well does not go back to the Greek original. Additionally, this may well mean that there is editing elsewhere as well: it is always difficult, when we have only a single manuscript not even in the original language of the work in question, to know how close a text is to its first edition. So we need to be cautious about assuming that everything in our text here goes back to the Greek original.

THE CONSEQUENCES OF THE DATE

One result of the *Gospel of Judas* coming from the mid-second century is that at the time of its composition all the eyewitnesses of the events involving Jesus and Judas were long dead. Although it is far too simplistic to say that the accuracy of historical documents is in direct proportion to how near they are in time to the events, useful testimony must ultimately go back to contemporaneous people and artefacts. (Perhaps one should also add animals, as in the cases of the horse in Dorothy L. Sayers's *Have His Carcase*, the dog in Agatha Christie's *Dumb Witness*, and of course Conan Doyle's famous 'dog in the night-time'.) But with the *Gospel of Judas* we have no way of knowing whether the author had any direct contact with sources— animal, vegetable, or mineral—which go back to the time of the real Judas and the real Jesus.

On the other hand, the overwhelming consensus is that the four New Testament Gospels were written within roughly sixty years of Jesus' death. It is important to recognize that in these first two generations after the ministry of Jesus disciples who had known him—who had been participants in, and witnesses to, the drama of his life, death. and resurrection—were still alive.[9] A number of the characters in the Gospel narratives, disciples such as Peter, or those healed by Jesus, or his family members, would have gone on to play an active role in the early Church. They would have contributed their accounts of Jesus to the pool of material drawn upon by the Gospel writers. To take an example in connection with a specific incident, the man who carried Jesus' cross for him is named 'Simon of Cyrene, the father of Alexander and Rufus' (Mark 15: 21). As scholars often note, Mark almost certainly mentions this detail because he expected some of his readers to know these sons, who were— no doubt—proud narrators of their father's deed.[10] Additionally, Mark's account of the crucifixion refers to 'women looking on from afar, among whom were Mary Magdalene, Mary the mother of James the less and Joses, and Salome' (Mark 15: 40); again, as scholars frequently comment, this suggests that they provided eyewitness testimony for the account.[11] The author of Luke's Gospel talks explicitly about his sources when he writes about making use of the testimony of the 'eyewitnesses and servants of the word' having been passed down to him (Luke 1: 2).

In addition to this positive role of these eyewitnesses they would also probably have had the negative function of keeping in check tendencies to invent new traditions about Jesus. In Chapter 3 we saw how in the *second* century CE there is much more of a free-for-all as far as describing the events surrounding the life of Jesus is concerned: in Papias, for example, the legend develops in which Judas becomes an ogre of superhuman size and subhuman personal hygiene.

The line between the first and second centuries is of course completely arbitrary, the product of a decision to construct the calendar as it is. But there is a real difference between the period in which the four canonical Gospels were written (which finishes at roughly the end of the first century) and the time when the *Gospel of Judas* was composed. The former was populated by those who had been contemporaries of Jesus and Judas, the latter was not.

A Multitude of Gospels of Jesus?

Following on from this it is necessary to correct the very misleading impressions created by some authors to the effect that there were numerous Gospels in earliest Christianity all of which are in the same historical boat. These Gospels all claim to represent accurately the teachings of Jesus, the story goes, but one party in the early Church managed to impose its picture of Jesus on us because it won the political struggle and suppressed all the competition. Bart Ehrman puts the case eloquently, if unconvincingly:

Rewriting History

There were lots of gospels. The four in the New Testament are anonymous writings—only in the second century did they come to be called by the names of Jesus' disciples (Matthew and John) and of two companions of the apostles (Mark the companion of Peter; and Luke the companion of Paul). Other gospels appeared that also claimed to be written by apostles. In addition to our newly discovered Gospel of Judas, we have gospels allegedly written by Philip and by Peter, two different gospels by Jesus' brother Judas Thomas, one by Mary Magdalene, and so on.

All of these gospels (and epistles, apocalypses, etc.) were connected with apostles, they all claimed to represent the true teachings of Jesus, and they were all revered—by one Christian group or another—as sacred scripture. As time went on, more and more started to appear. Given the enormous debates that were being waged over the proper interpretation of the religion, how were people to know which books to accept?

In brief, one of the competing groups in Christianity succeeded in overwhelming all the others. This group gained more converts than its opponents and managed to relegate all its competitors to the margins. This group decided what the Church's organizational structure would be. It decided which creeds Christians would recite. And it decided which books would be accepted as Scripture. This was the group to which Irenaeus belonged, as did other figures well known to scholars of second- and third-century Christianity, such as Justin Martyr and Tertullian. This group became 'orthodox,' and once it had sealed its victory over all of its opponents, it rewrote the history of the engagement—claiming that it had always been the majority opinion of Christianity, that its views had always been the views of the apostolic Churches and of the apostles, that its creeds were rooted directly in the teachings of Jesus. The books that it accepted as Scripture proved the point, for Matthew, Mark, Luke and John all tell the story as the proto-orthodox had grown accustomed to hearing it.[12]

So Ehrman's points here boil down to: (1) that there were a considerable number of Gospels sloshing around in the melting pot of earliest Christianity; (2) that the choice of the four New Testament Gospels boils down simply to the political triumph of the section of Christianity which championed them; and (3) that what this group did was ultimately to distort historical reality ('it rewrote the history'). So, far from actually being those who kept alive the true portrayal of Jesus, their work actually consisted in covering up what really happened.

But this story as it is spun by Ehrman runs into the difficulty that the four Gospels in the New Testament—as he himself admits—are the earliest portraits of Jesus.[13] So there appears to be some inconsistency in his view that the *earliest* documents in the case are the product of a *rewriting of history*. What is this history that pre-dates the four New Testament Gospels? The answer is, we do not have one, and we have no evidence either that the Church Fathers had one which they were so desperately trying to cover up.

Diversity Before Harmony?

A view which quite often goes hand-in-hand with that of Ehrman is the version of events put forward by Elaine Pagels, in her best-selling *The Gnostic Gospels*. As she puts it, there is no unified Church in the beginning which then subsequently develops all sorts of heresies and splinter groups; in fact, she maintains, it is the other way around:

Contemporary Christianity, diverse and complex as we find it, actually may show more unanimity than the Christian churches of the first and second centuries. For nearly all Christians since that time, Catholics,

Protestants, or Orthodox, have shared three basic premises. First, they accept the canon of the New Testament; second, they confess the apostolic creed; and third, they affirm specific forms of church institution. But every one of these—the canon of Scripture, the creed, and the institutional structure—emerged in its present form only toward the end of the second century. Before that time, as Irenaeus and others attest, numerous gospels circulated among various Christian groups, ranging from those of the New Testament, Matthew, Mark, Luke, and John, to such writings as the *Gospel of Thomas*, the *Gospel of Philip*, and the *Gospel of Truth*, as well as many other secret teachings, myths, and poems attributed to Jesus or his disciples. Some of these apparently, were discovered at Nag Hammadi; many others are lost to us. Those who identified themselves as Christians entertained many— and radically differing—religious beliefs and practices. And the communities scattered throughout the known world organized themselves in ways that differed widely from one group to another.

Yet by A.D. 200, the situation had changed ... [14]

So Pagels lumps the first two centuries together, classifying them as extremely diverse, with the next 1,800 years being relatively homogeneous. This is a little surprising. Not only are Pagels's 'three basic premises' questionable (Catholic, Orthodox, and Protestant are certainly not in complete agreement on 'the canon of Scripture, the creed, and the institutional structure') but, according to the World Christian Database, there are currently over 9,000 denominations worldwide (the various Churches of John Coltrane constituting some of the most unusual new entries).[15] Against this background Pagels's claims about 'the Christian churches of the first and second centuries' are probably exaggerated as an assessment of the second century. But to trace this diversity back to the *first* century as well is dangerously misleading.

Rewriting History

As we have already noted, the four New Testament Gospels are the only examples which can be confidently dated to before 100 CE, and they share—particularly when judged by their own standards rather than by currently important criteria such as canons, creeds, and officials—their most important concerns in common.[16] All four evangelists centre on Jesus' coming as Messiah in fulfilment of Old Testament promises, on his death and resurrection, and on the salvation which he accomplishes. On these focal points, there is little diversity.

However, in the early second century (again, when the eye-witnesses are a thing of the past), we begin to see Gospels emerging which sit rather more loosely to some of these central tenets, and which develop their own interests. The *Gospel of Thomas*, a work dating probably to around 120–140 CE, still sees Jesus as a saviour and revealer, but not by virtue of his death and resurrection and not in fulfilment of the scriptures.

So, in the beginning, there is clearly—at least according to the documents which have survived—unanimity on those central concerns of the four New Testament Gospels and this is then followed *later* by an explosion of Gospels many of which show Jesus in a very different light. Of this second-century tendency the *Gospel of Judas* is a prime example.

CONCLUSION

So even if we do not know why the *Gospel of Judas* was written, and how exactly it was used, the 'when' is more accessible. It is very probable that the book is influenced by the phraseology of the Gospel of Matthew, which would make the end of the first century CE the earliest possible date. But then the time-frame

147

is pushed further forward by the presence of the rather developed picture of the early Church's eucharist, which is already assumed in the work to be a kind of sacrifice. And forcing it later still are Gnostic ideas and deities which we only know of from the mid-second century onwards. So the mid–late second century is probably a fairly safe bet, and is even safer if our *Gospel of Judas* is the same as that mentioned by Irenaeus. Either way, this dating of the work is roughly the consensus view in any case.

However, what is misleading is the implied claim, sometimes found in the recent spate of literature, that the *Gospel of Judas* might be useful for reconstructing who Jesus really was. It is an empirical fact that there was a multitude of 'Gospels' in the first two centuries CE: that much is undeniably true. But a multitude of Gospels all with equal claim to be accurate testimony about Jesus? That is quite a different matter. To quote one final excerpt about the *Gospel of Judas* which goes off the rails at this point:

This gospel has a completely different understanding of God, the world, Christ, salvation, human existence—not to mention of Judas himself—than came to be embodied in the Christian creeds and canon. It will open up new vistas for understanding Jesus and the religious movement he founded.[17]

But as far as 'understanding Jesus' is concerned, will it? Really? I would be interested to hear if scholars have a concrete proposal for a single thing which the *Gospel of Judas* actually tells us about the real Jesus which does not already derive from the canonical writings.

The four New Testament Gospels are the only sources which have any real claim to be able to tell us about the real Judas Iscariot. As we saw in Chapter 2, the events of the betrayal are narrated in a very similar way in all four accounts, and so the chances are slim indeed of a different version which pops up a century later getting to the truth behind these much older reports. The same goes for the presentations of Jesus. Far from opening up 'new vistas for understanding Jesus', it is in fact the *Gospel of Judas* which—to turn Bart Ehrman's words against him—attempts to rewrite history.

7

Brave New World

Finally we come to assess the *ideas* in the *Gospel of Judas* and the view of reality which the text advocates. We have already seen that there has been a great deal of excitement about the apparent diversity of earliest Christianity, and about the variety of views held about Jesus in the second century. Our previous chapter mentioned Herb Krosney's conclusion: 'If an entire sect believed that the great betrayal had in fact been ordered by Jesus and carried out by his favored disciple, that interpretation could, after study, become as valid as the version told in the New Testament.'[1] So does the *Gospel of Judas* have a claim to this? We have already seen that the historical foundations of the *Gospel of Judas*'s reports about Jesus are decidedly shaky. But does it nevertheless offer a spiritual vision of Jesus as compelling as that of the New Testament? This chapter will summarize briefly the system of thought expressed in the *Gospel of Judas*, and offer a theological evaluation of it.

A SKETCH OF THE THEOLOGY OF THE *GOSPEL OF JUDAS*

One of the traditional ways to order a theological system is to follow the sequence: God—creation—sin—redemption—end-times; something like this structure is found, for example, in John Calvin's famous *Institutes of the Christian Religion*. But for a theological system like that of the *Gospel of Judas* it may be better to follow a set of questions with a more native Gnostic logic:

> Now it is not merely the washing which liberates, but also the knowledge (*gnōsis*): Who were we and what have we become? Where were we and where are we now cast? Whither are we hastening and from what have we been delivered? What is birth? What is rebirth? (Theodotus, cited in Clement of Alexandria, *c*.200 CE)[2]

Some of the questions raised here in this classic articulation of Gnostic concerns will serve as our structure as we flesh out the theology of the *Gospel of Judas.*

Who were We? Where were We?

From the creation account which Jesus reveals to Judas we know that ultimately everything derives from the great light-cloud (codex, p. 47), and yet in the course of the successive creations the light has become increasingly diluted. But even though some heavenly entities may have had their light quenched by ignorance, Seth and his descendants will survive and indeed triumph: they are accompanied by the cloud of knowledge (pp. 50–1) which will ensure this. As far as the individual members of this holy generation are concerned, their true divine 'selves' have pre-existed their bodily incarnations. The real person in every Gnostic is a spark of light from the eternal heavenly sphere.

Brave New World

What have We Become? Where are We Now Cast?

These heavenly souls, however, have found their way into physical bodies in the material cosmos. This world is full of those who are deficient in heavenly light and knowledge, and who have come under the sway of Saklas and the heavenly archons and stars which dictate the world's course (pp. 45–6). The most ignorant among humanity seem to be those who have come under the influence of the false priests, the leaders of the 'orthodox' Church (pp. 38–40). Given this setting of deficiency and ignorance, those who really know themselves and understand the nature of the world are perhaps doomed to a temporary mood of grief, as was the case for Judas (pp. 35, 46, 57). No better than the ignorant company which the Gnostic has in the world is the physical body, created by a foolish demiurge, in which the spiritual soul is stuck. All these inconveniences are, however, temporary for the seed of Seth.

Whither are We Hastening?

The end of time is a major theme in the *Gospel of Judas*, principally in the two dialogues either side of the long monologue of Jesus in Part II of the work. The first image of the Gnostic's future salvation is that of resurrection (p. 43)—not, of course, of the body in which the soul is imprisoned, but rather a resurrection in which the soul is set free both from its captivity in the material world, as well as from the danger of being deceived by hostile powers.

This liberation seems to lie at the heart of the *Gospel of Judas*'s conception of salvation: becoming part of the 'indomitable' or 'kingless' realm (p. 45). This will ultimately be accomplished when—after a final outbreak of sin at the end of time (p. 54)—there is a judgment of the wicked (p. 40), Saklas's influence comes to end (p. 54), and the deceiving stars will perish (p. 55). After this, the holy generation of Seth will take up residence with the angels in a huge house topped with lush vegetation—an image of a paradisal palace (p. 45).

'Not Merely the Washing, but also the Knowledge ...'

Although scholars also draw attention to the ritual component in Gnostic faith and practice, it is by and large the knowledge, or *gnōsis*, which is the centre of attention in the primary sources.[3] And in this the *Gospel of Judas* is no exception. Part of the answer to the question 'what is rebirth' posed above is seen in the *Gospel of Judas* in the gradual progress which Judas makes from being in the same boat as the other disciples, to his eventual ascent into the cloud of light: the journey is made through his apprehension of the special knowledge revealed to him by Jesus. The whole plan of the *Gospel of Judas* shows that in this respect it is a prime example of a 'Gnostic' work.

THEOLOGICAL EVALUATION

Having explored the *Gospel of Judas* both line by line in Chapter 4 and in the thematic sketch above, we can now assess the content. In order to do this, some of the key characteristics of Jesus from both the *Gospel of Judas* and the canonical Gospels will be picked out and examined in parallel. As was mentioned in the Introduction, we will be scrutinizing not only the *Gospel of Judas* here, but also the claims made on its behalf by some of its new-found admirers.

Jesus Without the Old Testament

All four of the New Testament Gospel writers present Jesus' life, death, and resurrection as happening in fulfilment of the Old Testament scriptures. As the Apostle Paul also put it: 'For I passed on to you as of first importance what I also received: that Christ died for our sins in accordance with the Scriptures, that he was buried, and that he was raised on the third day according to the Scriptures...' (1 Cor. 15: 3–4). Mark's Gospel, after its opening sentence, begins with two Old Testament quotations which set the scene for John the Baptist and Jesus. Matthew starts his Gospel with a genealogy which shows that Jesus is the goal of the family lines of Abraham and David, and goes on to present Jesus as the fulfilment of Old Testament prophecy five times in the first two chapters alone.[4] Again, Jesus is the redeeming descendant of Abraham and David in the first chapter of Luke's Gospel (Luke 1: 72–4, 69), and the opening chapter of John strikes a similar note: 'Philip found Nathanael and said to him, "We have found the one of whom Moses in the Law and also the prophets wrote, Jesus of Nazareth, the son of Joseph."' (John 1: 45).

The very same themes crop up again at the *ends* of each of the stories. Jesus' crucifixion is most often seen as fulfilling the Old Testament Psalms, as is his betrayal by Judas. We saw in Chapter 2 that alongside pronouncing the woe upon Judas that it would have been better for him never to have been born, Jesus says nevertheless that 'the Son of Man will go as it is *written* about him'.[5]

In this context, the single most important Old Testament passage for these early Christian writers was Psalm 41:

> My enemies speak evil of me:
> 'When will he die and his name perish?'
> If one comes to see me, his heart utters vain words,
> while he gathers iniquity for himself;
> when he goes out, he talks all about it.
> All who hate me whisper together against me;
> they plan the worst for me.
> They say, 'An ill fate is poured out on him;
> when he lies down, he will not rise again.'
> Even my close friend in whom I have put my trust,
> who ate my bread, has kicked his heel against me.
>
> (Psalm 41: 5–9)

This section of the Psalm begins, then, with the plotting of enemies, but lends itself particularly well to being taken as a reference to Judas because of the last two lines. Mark's reference to this Psalm is certainly the most muted, but he does appear to record an allusion to it by Jesus: 'And as they were reclining at table and eating, Jesus said, "Truly, I say to you, one of you who is eating with me will betray me."' (Mark 14: 18). A number of scholars, such as James Robinson in his Judas book, suspect a reference to Psalm 41 here.[6] What is implicit in Mark, however, is explicit in John's Gospel, where the last line of the excerpt above is cited: 'The Scripture is to be fulfilled, "He who has eaten my bread has lifted his heel against me."' (John 13: 18). In fact, in the book of Acts, when Peter comments in the first sermon there that David in the Psalms prophesied about Judas, it seems that he can take for granted that the audience knows exactly what he is talking about:

In those days Peter stood up in the midst of the brothers (the crowd of people was about 120 altogether) and said, 'Brothers, the Scripture which the Holy Spirit spoke in advance by the mouth of David concerning Judas, who became a guide to those who arrested Jesus, had to be fulfilled.' (Acts 1: 15–16)

All this shows, among other things, that with the four New Testament evangelists we are in a world in close touch with early Judaism, a world saturated with the Old Testament. They saw Jesus' life, death, and resurrection as the fulfilment of the Scriptures, and regarded these Scriptures as the indispensable guide to the interpretation of Jesus' activity. In this, they were continuing the thought-patterns of Jesus, who himself constantly quoted Israel's Bible and used it to explain his actions. He saw the Law and the Prophets as supplying the script for the drama of his ministry.

So for anyone familiar with the literature of the Old and New Testaments, and of early Judaism, reading the *Gospel of Judas* is like entering a different world. The ideas of 'scripture' and of 'fulfilment', as well as actual quotations from the Old Testament, are completely absent. In fact, they are more than just absent.

Jesus and the Biblical God

Far from being indifferent to the Old Testament and its God, the *Gospel of Judas* is positively hostile to YHWH, the one God who is creator and ruler of all things in the Old and New Testaments.

The *Gospel of Judas* takes supremacy away from the biblical God, and gives it to the supreme Gnostic deity, the 'Great Invisible Spirit', described by Judas as 'the one whose name I am not worthy to speak' (codex, p. 35). There are several instances of polemic against the God of the Old and New Testaments.

It is creation in particular which is recast as the activity of 'Saklas', the evil deity: 'Then Saklas said to his angels, "Let us make man according to the likeness and according to the image." And they created Adam and his wife Eve—who in the cloud is called Zoe' (p. 52). In the Gnostic scheme of things, Saklas is the biblical god, and yet —as we have seen—is an evil figure. He is a god with a temporary career, even though in the present he receives the sacrifices of the unenlightened. It is this deity, then, who is cast as the maker of humanity, a second-rate demiurge rather than (as is the case in the Bible) the supreme God.

This contrast is an extremely important one in the *Gospel of Judas* because the worship of Saklas practised by unredeemed humanity is set directly in opposition to the true act of service performed by Judas. Just as the other disciples are pictured as whisky priests, so Judas is described as the high priest *par excellence*, who will offer the ultimate sacrifice of the body of Jesus: 'You will sacrifice the man who carries me about' (p. 56). The world of difference between these two priesthoods results from the respective objects of worship: the low-grade god Saklas on the one hand as opposed (probably) to the Great Invisible Spirit on the other.

Overall, the picture of the biblical God in the *Gospel of Judas* is—from the standpoint of Christian tradition—nothing short of blasphemous. The God of the Old Testament has been dethroned to make room for the 'Great Invisible Spirit', is assigned only the most menial tasks in the elaborate Gnostic creation account, and is described as the foolish deity worshipped by the foolish generation of humanity which does not have *gnōsis*.

The Gospel of Judas and Jewish–Christian Relations

Despite this, some scholars have claimed that part of the payoff of the *Gospel of Judas* might be that, in taking it seriously, Christians will perhaps be able to re-examine the history of anti-Jewish prejudice. The idea is that since Judas has for some Christian theologians (from John Chrysostom and other Church Fathers like him to Karl Barth in the twentieth century) been the embodiment of everything that is wrong with Judaism, a reinterpretation of Judas can only be a good thing. As Marvin Meyer puts it:

In contrast to the New Testament gospels, Judas Iscariot is presented as a thoroughly positive figure in the Gospel of Judas, a role model for all those who wish to be disciples of Jesus. That is probably why the Gospel of Judas ends with the story of the betrayal of Jesus and not the crucifixion of Jesus. The point of the gospel is the insight and loyalty of Judas as the paradigm of discipleship. In the end, he does exactly what Jesus wants. In the biblical tradition, however, Judas—whose name has been linked to 'Jew' and 'Judaism'—was often portrayed as the evil Jew who turned Jesus in to be arrested and killed, and thereby the biblical figure of Judas the Betrayer has fed the flames of anti-Semitism. Judas in the present gospel may counteract this anti-Semitic tendency.[7]

One of the problems in this argument consists of the sloppy merging of 'the biblical tradition' with later Christian thought in which Judas was the archetypal Jew, and this means that the final sentence has no real basis to it. Herb Krosney follows the same tack, commenting that: 'The Gospel of Judas offers no blood libel that will course through history, causing vilification of Jews, pogroms, and even the Holocaust.'[8] No, the *Gospel of Judas* does not, but it does say that the god of Jews is a fool (as per his name 'Saklas'), a god falsely worshipped, and whose influence in the world is only temporary. This is one reason why the importance Krosney attaches to the *Gospel of Judas* seems rather exaggerated in the conclusion to his book:

I hope that the knowledge we gain will help to promote understanding of those earlier times when Christianity diverged from its Judaic origins, and that it will somehow bring not a sense of betrayal, not a breaking of faith, but an increased sense of brotherhood on this increasingly crowded planet.[9]

The paradox here, however, is that it is the earlier, New Testament Gospels which root Jesus properly in the Jewish world in which he lived. The *Gospel of Judas*, on the other hand, may mitigate some of the unpleasantness of the betrayal, but in the course of doing so it creates a Jesus totally detached from his real Jewish origins. The difficulty for those who champion Gnostic accounts of Jesus is that these Gnostic Gospels consistently make this move, reinventing Christianity as a religion which need not be rooted in the Hebrew scriptures. But to imagine that Christians could somehow get on better with Jews by downgrading the Old Testament is slightly peculiar. The fact is that no Christianity worthy of the name can abandon the Old Testament and its God, and yet this is precisely what the *Gospel of Judas* does.

Brave New World

Jesus and the Apostles

As with the Old Testament, so also with the New. We have seen that one of the central premises of the *Gospel of Judas* is that its message is not fundamentally public truth witnessed by the apostles and proclaimed, but knowledge secretly revealed to Judas. As the prologue says, it is 'the secret message of the revelation which Jesus spoke to Judas Iscariot'. As such, the *Gospel of Judas* attempts to supersede the New Testament Gospels at the outset by its claim to be secret revelation, and then later on by the aspersions it casts on the other disciples.

First, however, the consensus of the earliest witnesses is that Jesus' life, death, and resurrection took place in the public domain. As Paul in the book of Acts says of the whole business, 'it was not done in a corner' (Acts 26: 26). A 'corner' in ancient Greek (and Latin) parlance is a metaphor for a discreet, secluded place. In one of Plato's dialogues, the character Callicles advances the theory that old men who continue to indulge in philosophy at their age deserve a whipping: they should not be avoiding 'the centres and market-places of the city' and preferring to spend their time 'in a corner'. Epictetus, a first-century CE philosopher, talks about how dangerous it can be to pursue an argument in Rome if one antagonizes a rich man of consular rank, rather than merely disputing 'in a corner'.[10] So Paul in the Acts of the Apostles stresses that the events of Jesus' life are a matter of public record.

Similarly, in all four Gospels, Jesus' ministry is described as having been pursued in public places, and this is emphasized in John's Gospel: 'Jesus answered him, "I have spoken openly to the world. I have always taught in the synagogue and in the temple, where all Jews come together. I have said nothing in secret."' (John 18: 20). Jesus did teach that there was a distinction between those who failed to understand his message and those whose eyes were opened by God.[11] But in terms of the content of his message, his Gospel, it was nothing other than what he taught in the synagogues and in the temple. Jesus does spend time privately with his disciples as well, but even there we do not find him communicating secret revelation to individuals. The focus is on what he says out in the open.

Secondly, just as important as the public context of Jesus' teaching is that the recipients of the revelation, who then go on to testify to it, are very much a *plural* group. In this context, the words 'us' and 'we' occur frequently in the Gospels and elsewhere in the New Testament, because the truth about Jesus is regarded as having been committed not to an individual, but to a group:

Inasmuch as many have undertaken to draw up an account of the things that have been fulfilled among us ... (Luke 1: 1)

The Word became flesh and dwelt among us, and we have seen his glory ... (John 1: 14)

That which was from the beginning, which we have heard, which we have seen with our eyes, which we have looked at and our hands have touched ... (1 John 1: 1)

At many times and in various ways in the past God spoke to our forefathers through the prophets but in these last days he has spoken to us by the Son, whom he appointed heir of all things, and through whom he made the worlds. (Heb. 1: 1–2)

So the apostolic teaching is plural witness to public revelation. The very different character of revelation in the *Gospel of Judas*, however, means it has additional problems associated with it.

Principally, in abandoning the plural witness of the apostles to public events, there would have been no way for those of the time to establish what Jesus had taught and what he had not. An interesting situation from the *Gospel of Mary* may illustrate this. In this Gnostic Gospel, Mary recounts what she claims is a private revelation to her from Jesus; the disciples Andrew and Peter dispute that it comes from Jesus, whereas Mary, supported by Levi, maintains the genuineness of the message.[12] But how does any of the characters apart from Mary know the truth of the matter? Since Gnostic revelation does take place precisely 'in a corner', it is inevitably—in contrast to the plural nature of the apostolic testimony—one person's word against another. This is also the case with the *Gospel of Judas*, where we have the same difficulties associated with the claim to be a secret revelation to one of the disciples—a problem which never arises in the New Testament Gospels. Indeed, the importance of the plurality of the witness is encapsulated in the *fourfold* nature of the Gospel which was eventually canonized.

A Disembodied Jesus

'You will sacrifice the man who carries me about' (codex, p. 56). We have already looked at this portentous statement for what it tells us about Judas. But it also says a good deal about how the *Gospel of Judas* understands Jesus, revealing that he is not a human being as such, but a divine spirit carried in a body which he can speak of as not really belonging to himself. The image is of a person being borne along: we saw in Chapter 4 one ancient example which uses the original Greek word in connection with a horse 'carrying about' its rider.

Theologians conventionally label this view of Jesus as 'docetic' (from the Greek word *dokein*, meaning 'to seem', 'to appear'), because Jesus only *appears* to be human. This is a development which clearly post-dates Jesus himself, as well— almost certainly—as the earliest Jewish believers in Jesus: it is very difficult to imagine a detachment of Jesus' essence from his physical body being envisaged on Jewish soil, even if it is possible that this idea had arisen by the end of the first century CE.[13] Although some people in antiquity evidently found a non-human Jesus appealing, it is difficult to imagine how this might prove popular in the modern theological climate: conservatives will always continue to insist on the divine and human natures of Jesus, and those of a more revisionist persuasion tend to champion Jesus' humanity, rather than undermine it. Not only does detaching Jesus from his body lead to a completely different conception of salvation from that underlying orthodox pictures (most of which draw heavily on the principle that if God does not take on humanity then that humanity is not redeemed), most Christians of almost any theological position would find the idea of a non-human Jesus pastorally uninviting to say the least.

A Loveless Jesus

A disturbing feature of the *Gospel of Judas* is one which has— surprisingly—not been noted by any of the first round of works on the text: the absence of *love*. There is no reference to the love of God or of Jesus, or of love as something which should characterize the disciples of Jesus. This is not confined merely to the absence of the word; there is also nothing in the *Gospel of*

Judas which could easily be described as showing divine love at work.

When we look at the four canonical Gospels, and at the New Testament as a whole, the picture could hardly be more different. Beginning with Mark's Gospel, the first scene in which Jesus appears (his baptism) shows the love of the Father for the Son: 'And a voice came from heaven: "You are my Son, whom I love; in you I am well pleased." ' (Mark 1: 11). Still in the first chapter, Jesus' love is then evident when he is described as 'filled with compassion' for a leper. Disregarding the conventional attitude to such people, he touches the leper and heals him (Mark 1: 40–42).

Again, when Jesus saw the large crowd in the scene leading up to the feeding of the five thousand, 'he had compassion on them, because they were like sheep without a shepherd ... ' (Mark 6: 34). And so on and so on. The culmination of this in Mark's Gospel is Jesus' willingness to go to his death for the sake of the salvation of others: 'For even the Son of Man came not to be served, but to serve, and to give his life as a ransom for many' (Mark 10: 45). When the critical moment of testing comes in the Garden of Gethsemane he accepts his destiny and goes through with the divine purpose. And all this stress on the love of God in Jesus is to be reflected in the human responses to it: Jesus comments that the Old Testament commands to love God and love neighbour are the most important of all the laws (Mark 12: 28–31).

Almost all of this is reproduced in the Gospels of Matthew and Luke which as we saw in Chapter 2 draw heavily on Mark as a source. Two examples of additional material in Matthew show how the emphasis on love is developed further; his is the only Gospel to include Jesus' offer of rest for the weary:

'Come to me, all you who are weary and heavy-laden, and I will give you rest. Take my yoke upon you and learn from me, for I am meek and humble in heart, and you will find rest for your souls. For my yoke is easy and my burden is light.' (Matt. 11: 28–30)

In the Sermon on the Mount, radical love is integral to Christian discipleship. Jesus takes the Old Testament commandment to 'love your neighbour' and resists the interpretation which had been put upon it by some of his contemporaries, namely, that it meant: love those close to you but despise those who are not in your in-group. Rather, for Jesus, *everyone* is a neighbour: 'You have heard that it was said, "Love your neighbour and hate your enemy." But I say to you: Love your enemies and pray for those who persecute you.' (Matt. 5: 43–44).

Again, two well-known parables from Luke's Gospel which are not in the other Gospels will serve to highlight some of Luke's distinctiveness. The Parable of the Prodigal Son focuses on the love of God, with the father in the story representing God and the lost son sinful humanity. The story which Jesus tells involves two sons, one of whom asked his father for his share of the inheritance in advance. The son then went off and 'wasted his substance with riotous living', as the Authorized Version puts it (Luke 15: 13). Then, owing to famine, he suddenly found himself in poverty and starvation, and so returned to his father: 'But while he was still a long way off, his father saw him and was filled with compassion for him. He ran to his son, threw his arms around him and kissed him' (Luke 15: 20). The point here, then, is the way in which God goes out to seek lost humanity out of love, and this despite the prodigal's previous disregard for his father. On the other side, the Parable of the Good Samaritan, with its focus on practical love for those whom one would prefer not to help, is a call to radical love on the part of disciples: 'Go and do likewise' (Luke 10: 37).

But the theme of love is most prominent in John's Gospel. To draw attention to one distinctive feature of this Gospel it is striking that the love of Father, Son, and disciples is particularly tightly bound one to another in Jesus' teaching: 'Whoever has my commandments and keeps them is one who loves me. He who loves me will be loved by my Father, and I will love him and reveal myself to him' (John 14: 21). And the idea then appears pithily in the following chapter, 'Just as the Father has loved me, so also have I loved you' (John 15: 9).

Our focus here is on the Gospels, but the Epistles in the New Testament drive home the point again. The Apostle Paul's whole life is shaped by his conviction of the love of Christ: 'I no longer live myself, but Christ lives in me. The life I live in the body, I live by faith in the Son of God, who loved me and gave himself for me' (Gal. 2: 20). But perhaps the most wonderful exposition in all the New Testament comes in the work which has the famous statement 'God is love', the First Epistle of John:

Dear friends, let us love one another, for love comes from God, and everyone who loves is born of God and knows God. Whoever does not love does not know God, because God is love. By this the love of God is made known among us: God sent his one and only Son into the world so that we might live through him. This is love: not that we loved God, but that he loved us and sent his Son as an atoning sacrifice for our sins. Dear friends, since God so loved us, we also ought to love one another. No one has ever seen God; but if we love one another, God lives in us and his love is made complete in us. (1 John 4: 7–12)

All of this sort of talk is conspicuous by its absence from the *Gospel of Judas* in which Jesus treats his disciples with contemptuous disdain and laughs at the prospect of the destruction of fallen heavenly entities (codex, pp. 36, 55). (Although sometimes Jesus notes that he is not laughing at the disciples, or at Judas, this is not always the case.) These passages about laughter have been spun in an attempt to show that the Jesus of the *Gospel of Judas* is much more of a swell guy than the Jesus of the New Testament: Krosney, for example, claims that 'Jesus appears to be a less suffering, more joyful figure than in the canonical Gospels, and he has the capacity to laugh'.[14] Or again, 'Jesus [in the *Gospel of Judas*] is not a tormented figure who will die in agony on the cross. Instead, he is a friendly and benevolent teacher with a sense of humor.'[15]

But in the *Gospel of Judas* Jesus does not really come across like this. His laughter is actually the scornful laughter often evident in Gnostic literature—the laughter of one who is actually *detached* from the world, who stands above it in supercilious and mocking contempt. In fact, the Jesus of the New Testament is a much more down-to-earth figure than his disembodied Gnostic counterpart: in the canonical Gospels, he was persecuted by some of his more fastidious contemporaries as 'a friend of tax-collectors and sinners', and even labelled 'a glutton and a drunkard' (Matt. 11: 19/Luke 7: 34). The attempt to spin the *Gospel of Judas* again will not work because it is attempting to argue for the very opposite of what the sources say.

In fact, this spin is just one example of a common phenomenon in some of the recent literature on Gnosticism. Roger Bagnall, Professor of Classics at Columbia University, has described this view (which he does not endorse) well: 'The gnostics are validated as a direction in which Christianity could have gone and which would have made it warmer and fuzzier, much nicer than this cold orthodoxy stuff.'[16] On this account, who could fail to prefer this warm fuzziness of Gnosticism to the allegedly doctrinaire religion of John and Paul in the New Testament? But despite the attempts of some to push this line, it just will not work. The contrast—seen most divertingly in *The Da Vinci Code*—is historical fantasy, and should be given a decent burial. As we noted in the commentary on the *Gospel of Judas* earlier, religion for our author has a good deal of mystery, but is a loveless business.

A Jesus Without Suffering

Finally, closely connected to the New Testament themes of Jesus' embodied incarnation and his love is the importance of his suffering. The idea of a Jesus who escapes suffering may be appealing to some, but it hardly fits well with Jesus being the more earthly, human figure that he is in, for example, Krosney's account. The Jesus of the *Gospel of Judas* is not a person who shares in the world's suffering, but one who in splendid isolation is detached from it. In the New Testament, by contrast, Jesus' suffering and death are central themes, highlighted again and again in its different constituent books.

One reason for this is that suffering is considered to be integral to Christian discipleship, an inevitable way in which those who follow Jesus will end up imitating their master:

... to know him, and the power of his resurrection, and partnership in his sufferings, becoming conformed to him in his death. (Phil 3: 10)

For to this you were called, because Christ suffered for you, leaving you an example, that you should follow in his steps. (1 Pet. 2: 21)

Oddly enough, in the *Gospel of Judas* suffering does seem to be part and parcel of Judas's experience—'grieving' and being 'cursed' crop up frequently (codex, pp. 35, 46, 57; 47). But suffering is not something which sullies Jesus himself. As such, we have the 'loyalty of Judas as the paradigm of discipleship' being highlighted, but this has nothing to do with the character and life of Jesus himself as something to be followed.[17] Discipleship in the *Gospel of Judas* is apparently merely a matter of obeying Jesus' instructions.

But the principal reason for the focus on Jesus' suffering in the New Testament is that it is the solution to human sin and divine judgment. We have already seen as much in the teaching of Jesus about his death in Chapter 2: 'For even the Son of Man came not to be served but to serve, and to give his life as a ransom for many' (Mark 10: 45). In the fourth Gospel, similarly, this idea is also part of the testimony of John the Baptist about Jesus: 'Behold, the Lamb of God, who takes away the sin of the world!' (John 1: 29).

This strand of the Gospels' teaching was also central to that of the epistles. To take a smattering of examples from the rest of the New Testament:

'For I passed on to you as of first importance what I also received: that Christ died for our sins in accordance with the Scriptures, that he was buried, and that he was raised on the third day according to the Scriptures . . . ' (1 Cor. 15: 3–4)

And just as it is allotted to people to die once, and after that to face judgment, so also Christ was sacrificed once to take away the sins of many people; and he will appear a second time, sinless, to bring salvation to those who are waiting for him. (Heb. 9: 27–8)

For Christ suffered for sins once for all, the righteous for the unrighteous, in order to bring you to God. (1 Pet. 3: 18)

He is the atoning sacrifice for our sins, and not only for ours but also for the sins of the whole world. (1 John 2: 2)

The New Testament is full of this language celebrating the coming of Jesus and his suffering. Far from being merely a tragic and gloomy affair, the death of Jesus and the salvation from sin and judgment which he has brought about are a part of the divine plan and a function of Jesus' love. As we have seen, Paul rejoiced in his saviour who, he says, 'loved me and gave himself for me' (Gal. 2: 20).

In the apocalyptic language of the book of Revelation, this event is an occasion for the heavenly figures there to sing in praise of Jesus:

> And they sang a new song:
> 'Worthy are you to take the scroll
> and to open its seals,
> because you were slain,
> and with your blood you purchased for God
> people from every tribe and language and people and nation.'
>
> (Rev. 5: 9)

I wonder whether the *Gospel of Judas* can really give us anything to sing about. We have seen two principal themes running through this chapter. There is the criticism of the biblical creator God, derided as an unsavoury deity; the attitudes in the *Gospel of Judas* to the Old Testament and to the apostles flow naturally from this. Then there are the interconnected themes of Jesus' disembodied nature and consequent lack of suffering.

Given that he is described this way in the *Gospel of Judas*, there is no sense of an identification of Jesus with humanity, or of Jesus' love for the world. Both the English word 'Gospel' and the Greek term for it (*euangelion*) mean 'good news', but I doubt whether this particular Gospel—journalistic and scholarly hype notwithstanding—really lives up to its name.

Epilogue
The Future of the *Gospel of Judas*

According to the New Testament Gospels, Jesus' death 'as a ransom for many' was, strange as it may sound, part of his intention and part of God's plan. Judas is accordingly presented as paradoxically fulfilling his role in this divine purpose, even though his action of handing over the innocent Jesus to the authorities was in itself an act of wickedness. The portraits of Judas from the second century then go off in various different directions. The comments on Judas in the Apostolic Fathers and early apocryphal writings, while keeping to the spirit of the New Testament, begin to turn him into a cautionary tale. Some in the emerging Gnostic movements view him in a completely different light and see the disciples as earthly reflections of the heavenly 'aeons', and Judas as connected with the—very significant—twelfth aeon.

Judas's own Gospel is now added to the melting pot of second-century portrayals of him. It is fairly clear that this new Gospel really does belong to the second century rather than to the first: in Chapter 6 we saw that the *Gospel of Judas* makes use of Matthew's Gospel, presumes a picture of a mainstream Church with a highly developed practice of the eucharist, and contains Greek names and Gnostic themes aplenty such as we first see appearing elsewhere in the second century.

Because of this, the *Gospel of Judas* certainly provides us with another window into the strange and turbulent world of second-century Gnosticism and Christianity. It is abundantly clear that the work reflects the bitter struggle over the identity of Jesus in that period. But as far as the period the *Gospel of Judas* purports to describe is concerned it does not tell us anything that we did not already know: it offers us no fresh insight into who Jesus and Judas really were, or into what happened in the events surrounding Jesus' death. The *Gospel of Judas* may be a catalyst for more careful analysis of the betrayal and passion of Jesus, but—as is the case with catalysts—it does not itself contribute anything to the proceedings.

Will the *Gospel of Judas* have a future in the popular imagination in the same way as, say, the Gospels of Thomas and Mary to some extent do? Or will it perhaps be consigned after a few months or years to the ranks of little-known Gnostic works such as the *Hypostasis of the Archons* and the *Trimorphic Protennoia*? Having 'Judas' in the title will certainly help to ensure its survival—indeed it may well become the best known of the apocryphal Gospels. The more important question concerns what sort of a role it will play in future debates over the identity of Jesus and the nature of earliest Christianity. Will it continue to be grist to the mill of those who see the distinction between the New Testament Gospels and the others as merely a result of orthodoxy's political victory? Or will it serve as an excellent illustration of some of the shifts which took place in the second century, in which Jesus began in some circles to be seen less as a suffering messiah who died and rose again in accordance with

Old Testament Scripture, and more as a mouthpiece for secret revelation and saving *gnōsis*?

Probably both; but the former position, at least as we have seen it presented by writers such as Elaine Pagels and Bart Ehrman, involves a number of leaps of faith—despite presenting itself as the version of events which is more liberated from theological bias. On the other hand, the more conventional approach, while not as newsworthy as its revisionist counterpart perhaps, actually rests on a more solid historical foundation. The four Gospels in the New Testament are the only surviving Gospels which derive from the time period of the eyewitnesses of Jesus' ministry. Unsurprisingly, as the documents which most closely reflect the time and life-setting of Jesus, they present him as he had really been remembered—as someone who lived and breathed the Old Testament and knew himself to be playing a special role in its fulfilment, rather than as a thoroughly un-Jewish figure: disembodied, detached from the world, offering not love but knowledge.

Notes

[1] Canto xxxiv. 63. Dante, *The Divine Comedy*, i. *Hell.* trans. Dorothy L. Sayers (Harmondsworth: Penguin, 1949), 286.

[2] Bart Ehrman's comment is almost certainly accurate: 'Eventually there will be hundreds of scholarly books and articles written about the Gospel of Judas.' B. D. Ehrman, *The Lost Gospel of Judas Iscariot: A New Look at Betrayer and Betrayed* (New York: Oxford University Press, 2006), 100.

CHAPTER 1 OUT OF EGYPT

[1] H. Krosney, *The Lost Gospel: The Quest for the Gospel of Judas Iscariot* (Washington, DC: National Geographic, 2006), 212.

[2] A much fuller version can be found ibid. and parts of the story are filled out by James Robinson as well as by the contributors to the National Geographic *Gospel of Judas* volume, especially Rodolphe Kasser's essay 'The Story of Codex Tchacos and the Gospel of Judas'.

[3] Some authors give the number of pages as 62 or 64 (some give more than one count!), but Kasser's enumeration is presumably the most reliable: R. Kasser, 'The Story of Codex Tchacos and the Gospel

175

of Judas', in R. Kasser, M. Meyer, and G. Wurst (eds.), *The Gospel of Judas* (Washington, DC: National Geographic, 2006), 47–76 (49).

4 Ibid., 50 and 64.

5 Emmel's comments are found in Krosney, *The Lost Gospel*, 283 and 303.

6 Ibid., 304.

7 Ibid., 9–27; Emmel's comment in his report is quoted in J. M. Robinson, *The Secrets of Judas: The Story of the Misunderstood Judas and his Lost Gospel* (New York: HarperSanFrancisco, 2006), 120.

8 Stephen Emmel's report is reprinted in full in Robinson, *Secrets of Judas*, 117–20.

9 Ibid., 122.

10 According to Andrew Cockburn, Frieda Tchacos has revealed that the suggested sum of $300,000 is 'wrong, but in the neighborhood'. A. Cockburn, 'The Judas Gospel', *National Geographic* 209/9 (May 2006), 78–95 (93).

11 Krosney, *The Lost Gospel*, 175 and 165 respectively.

12 <http://www.michelvanrijn.nl> is van Rijn's current website, which also gives a link to his old site which ran into legal trouble.

13 Kasser, 'The Story of Codex Tchacos and the Gospel of Judas', 60–1.

14 Quoted in Krosney, *The Lost Gospel*, 231. For more on Kasser's reaction, see his 'The Story of Codex Tchacos and the Gospel of Judas', 47–8, 65.

15 Kasser, 'The Story of Codex Tchacos and the Gospel of Judas', 66.

16 James Robinson's anxieties about whether there was going to be a qualified papyrus conservator with sufficient expertise and access to do the job have proved—to put it kindly—unfounded (Robinson, *Secrets of Judas*, 170–1).

17 Quoted in Krosney, *The Lost Gospel*, 239 and 243.

18 Ibid., 264.

19 Ibid., 302.

20 Kasser, 'The Story of Codex Tchacos and the Gospel of Judas', 64.

[21] Quoted in Robinson, *Secrets of Judas*, 162.

[22] Ibid.

[23] Ibid., 143–4.

[24] An unnamed London dealer, as quoted ibid., 141.

[25] Kasser, 'The Story of Codex Tchacos and the Gospel of Judas', 62.

[26] Some of the other projects on which Kasser was working during this period can be seen in the International Association of Coptic Studies newsletters from these years: <http://rmcisadu.let.uniroma1.it/~iacs/nlindx.htm>.

[27] Mario Roberty, email to the author (4 May 2006).

[28] Available on DVD: *The Gospel of Judas* (Washington DC: National Geographic, 2006).

[29] Krosney, *The Lost Gospel*, 257.

[30] Ibid., 262.

[31] Ibid., 261.

CHAPTER 2 JUDAS IN THE NEW TESTAMENT

[1] G. Schwarz, *Jesus und Judas: Aramaistische Untersuchungen zur Jesus–Judas–Überlieferung der Evangelien und der Apostelgeschichte* (Stuttgart: Kohlhammer, 1988), 6–12.

[2] In fact, the later *Gospel of the Ebionites* (probably from the first half of the second century) has a list of disciples in which Judas is actually not last: the author leaves Matthew until last, because Matthew is the one emphasized.

[3] See W. D. Davies and D. C. Allison, *The Gospel according to St Matthew*, iii. *Matthew XIX–XXVIII* (International Critical Commentary; Edinburgh: T. & T. Clark, 1997), 509–10. To take just a few examples, it is translated as a command in the New English Bible, the Jerusalem Bible, and the New American Standard Bible, and as a question in the King James Version, the Lutherbibel, and the Geneva Bible.

[4] Eusebius, *Ecclesiastical History*, VI.14, 7.

[5] H. Maccoby, *Judas Iscariot and the Myth of Jewish Evil* (New York: The Free Press, 1992), 25.

[6] A. C. Thiselton, *The First Epistle to the Corinthians* (Grand Rapids, Mich.: Eerdmans, 2000), 1205.

[7] On this evidence see in particular W. Horbury, 'The Twelve and the Phylarchs', in id., *Messianism among Jews and Christians: Biblical and Historical Studies* (London/New York: Continuum, 2003), 157–88; J. M. Baumgarten, 'The Duodecimal Courts of Qumran, the Apocalypse, and the Sanhedrin', *Journal of Biblical Literature*, 95 (1976), 145–71.

[8] W. Klassen, *Judas: Betrayer or Friend of Jesus?* (London: SCM Press, 1996), 74.

[9] Ibid., 67.

[10] Ibid., 85.

[11] K. Barth, *The Church Dogmatics*, II/2: *The Doctrine of God* (Edinburgh: T. & T. Clark, 1957), 464.

[12] Klassen, *Judas*, 11.

CHAPTER 3 THE NEXT 100 YEARS

[1] *Similitudes* VIII, 6.4; IX, 19.1; Pliny, *Letters* 10.96.

[2] So in my view Vogler jumps the gun a little in saying that Judas is used for ethical exhortation in the Apostolic Fathers. If this is the case, it is only implicit. W. Vogler, *Judas Iskarioth: Untersuchungen zu Tradition und Redaktion von Texten des Neuen Testaments und ausserkanonischer Schriften* (Berlin: Evangelische Verlagsanstalt, 1983), 121–6, esp. 125.

[3] *Gospel of Philip* 60, 12 (*Nag Hammadi Library*, 146).

[4] G. C. Stead, 'The Valentinian Myth of Sophia', *Journal of Theological Studies*, 20 (1969), 75–104 (78). Although the language of

'transgression' might presuppose disobedience incurring guilt, this is not necessarily the case with Sophia's action: in several versions of the story it is more a matter of, as one scholar puts it, '[S]ophia's wanton if innocent act'. See A. Logan, *Gnostic Truth and Christian Heresy: A Study in the History of Gnosticism* (Edinburgh: T. & T. Clark, 1996), 117.

[5] See further 1.20.3–4. Then comes a more complicated discussion in which Irenaeus wonders whether they mean that Judas was not representing the aeon but her 'Enthymesis' (her unformed offspring) or, alternatively, her 'suffering' (1.20.5).

CHAPTER 4 TRANSLATION AND INTERPRETATION

[1] For the standard translation, see James M. Robinson (ed.), *The Nag Hammadi Library* (New York: HarperCollins, 1990), 126.

[2] *Book of Thomas the Contender*, 138, 1–4 (*Nag Hammadi Library*, 201).

[3] J. D. Turner, 'Book of Thomas the Contender', in Robinson (ed.), *Nag Hammadi Library*, 199–200.

[4] Valentinus, fragment 7, quoted in Hippolytus, *Refutation of All Heresies*, VI.42, 2. For other instances in the sources, see C. Markschies, *Valentinus Gnosticus? Untersuchungen zur valentinianischen Gnosis mit einem Kommentar zu den Fragmenten Valentins* (Tübingen: Mohr, 1992), 207–10.

[5] Cf. the New Testament, where Jesus is explicitly said to have called the disciples: 'Jesus called them' (Matt. 4: 22); 'he called them' (Mark 1: 20); 'he called his disciples and chose from them twelve, whom he named apostles' (Luke 6: 13).

[6] Celsus, *Alēthēs Logos*, cited in Origen, *Contra Celsum*, V.59.

[7] *Gospel of Thomas*, 13 (*Nag Hammadi Library*, 127– 8).

[8] The author here uses phraseology which the Coptic Old Testament uses of 'the word of the Lord' coming to prophets and patriarchs. See W. E. Crum, *A Coptic Dictionary* (Oxford: Clarendon Press, 1939), 579*b*.

[9] Kasser, Meyer, and Wurst, *Gospel of Judas*, 21 n. 10.

[10] Mark 8: 29/ Matt. 16: 16/ Luke 9: 20.

[11] Umberto Eco, *The Name of the Rose* (London: Secker and Warburg, 1983), 474.

[12] Ibid., 95.

[13] *Apocalypse of Peter*, 81, 15–24 (Robinson, *Nag Hammadi Library*, 377).

[14] See e.g. H. Krosney, *The Lost Gospel: The Quest for the Gospel of Judas Iscariot* (Washington, DC: National Geographic, 2006), 278.

[15] Robinson, *Nag Hammadi Library*, 134.

[16] C. L. Hancock, 'Negative Theology in Gnosticism and Neoplatonism', in R. T. Wallis (ed.), *Neoplatonism and Gnosticism* (Albany, N.Y.: SUNY Press, 1992), 167–86 (175). See also J. D. Turner, 'Time and History in Sethian Gnosticism', in Hans-Gebhard Bethge, Stephen Emmel, K. L. King, and I. Schletterer (eds.), *For the Children, Perfect Instruction. Studies in Honor of Hans-Martin Schenke* (Nag Hammadi and Manichaean Studies, 54; Leiden/Boston: Brill, 2002), 203–14.

[17] *Gospel of Thomas*, 13 (*Nag Hammadi Library*, 127–8).

[18] *Testimony of Truth*, 29.1–21 (*Nag Hammadi Library*, 449–50).

[19] The National Geographic translation takes this phrase as 'the deeds of their deficiency' rather than of slaughter; although 'slaughter' perhaps fits the context better, 'deficiency' is also possible (Kasser, Meyer, and Wurst, *The Gospel of Judas*, 26).

[20] M. Meyer, Introduction, ibid., 1–16 (6).

[21] R. Kasser, 'The Story of Codex Tchacos and the Gospel of Judas', ibid., 47–76 (75).

[22] On the latter, see Chapter 3. For the Platonic idea, see Plato, *Timaeus*, 42b.

[23] *Apocryphon of John*, II.21.9–12 (*Nag Hammadi Library*, 117). See A. H. B. Logan, *Gnostic Truth and Christian Heresy: A Study in the History of Gnosticism* (Edinburgh: T. & T. Clark, 1996), 223.

[24] Mark 4: 5, 16–17/Matt. 13: 5, 20–1/Luke 8: 6, 13.

[25] U.-K. Plisch, 'Das Evangelium des Judas', *Zeitschrift für antikes Christentum*, 10 (2006), 5–14 (10 n. 16).

[26] Although the prefix to the word is not the usual one in Coptic, 'evil' is probably preferable here to 'day'. The markings above the words 'Sun' and 'Moon' (as also 'Evil One') indicate that these figures are probably deities rather than merely astronomical phenomena.

[27] Again, the National Geographic translation of 'send it' is technically correct (Kasser, Meyer, and Wurst, *The Gospel of Judas*, 32), although the Coptic probably has a very small scribal error here, meaning that the original would probably have been 'twelve'.

[28] See above all Strabo, *Geography*, 16.1.5, and Diodorus Siculus, *History* II. 10. A useful survey of some of the ancient literature, with an excellent bibliography, can be found in J. Reade, 'Alexander the Great and the Hanging Gardens of Babylon', *Iraq*, 62 (2000), 195–217.

[29] The context in Gen. 37: 26 is totally different, and the question is in any case a very common one. See for example Job 21: 15; Ps 30: 9; Eccles. 5: 11; 6: 8; Mark 8: 36, and parallels; Rom. 3: 1.

[30] The word *nekbōk* has been taken to be a negative form by some ('you shall *not* go'), perhaps by emending the text to *nnekbōk*. But as it stands the word could be a conjunctive (and so mean a positive 'going'), as noted in Layton's grammar: B. Layton, *A Coptic Grammar*, 2nd edn. (Wiesbaden: Harrassowitz Verlag, 2004), §351 (p. 276), where *nek-* is a variant form of the 2nd person singular. Layton notes that this variant form occurs with the verb *bōk* which we have here.

[31] 1 Cor. 2: 9; Pseudo-Philo, *Biblical Antiquities*, 26: 13. On the history of this formula, the best discussions are K. Berger, 'Zur Diskussion über die Herkunft von I Kor. II.9', *New Testament Studies*, 24 (1978), 270–83, and C. M. Tuckett, 'Paul and Jesus Tradition. The Evidence of 1 Corinthians 2: 9 and Gospel of Thomas 17', in T. J. Burke

(ed.), *Paul and the Corinthians: Studies on a Community in Conflict: Essays in Honour of Margaret Thrall* (Leiden: Brill, 2003), 55–73.

[32] *Apocryphon of John*, II.2.25–4.10 (*Nag Hammadi Library*, 106–7). See also the Nag Hammadi text of *Allogenes* for a very similar depiction: *Allogenes*, 60.28–67.20 (*Nag Hammadi Library*, 497–9).

[33] See Meyer's useful discussion of Autogenes: M. Meyer, 'Judas and the Gnostic Connection', in Kasser, Meyer, and Wurst, *The Gospel of Judas*, 137–69 (esp. 143–8).

[34] On Adamas revealing eternal beings, see *The Three Steles of Seth*, 119.22–4, where he is described under the sobriquet 'Geradama(s)' (*Nag Hammadi Library*, 363).

[35] See Meyer, 'Judas and the Gnostic Connection', 137–69. For more of the primary sources, see A. F. J. Klijn, *Seth in Jewish, Christian and Gnostic Literature* (Leiden: Brill, 1977), 81–117.

[36] See Gen. 1: 4, 10, 12, 18, 25; then in Gen. 1: 31, after the creation of humanity, it is 'very good'.

[37] A. Logan, 'The Ultimate Betrayal: Reflections on the Coptic *Gospel of Judas*' (unpub. paper delivered at Postgraduate Study Day, University of Exeter, 2006).

[38] *Eugnostos*, III.85.3–9 (*Nag Hammadi Library*, 236). Cf. also *Gospel of the Egyptians*, III.60.4–5 (*Nag Hammadi Library*, 215), which talks of 'the virgins of the corrupt sowing of this aeon'.

[39] Jerome, *Liber interpretationis hebraicorum nominum*, 52.2 (Mic.) and 9.4 (Gen.) respectively: under 'Nemroth'.

[40] For the best treatment of the background to Nimrod here, see K. van der Toorn and P. W. van der Horst, 'Nimrod before and after the Bible', *Harvard Theological Review*, 83 (1990), 1–29.

[41] *Trimorphic Protennoia*, 39.21–7 (*Nag Hammadi Library*, 515).

[42] *Hypostasis of the Archons*, 95.7–8 (*Nag Hammadi Library*, 168).

[43] *Apocryphon of* John, II.11.16–22 (*Nag Hammadi Library*, 111); cf. *Gospel of the Egyptians*, III. 58.23–59.1 (*Nag Hammadi Library*, 215). On the motif of Saklas's boast, see N. A. Dahl, 'The Arrogant

Archon and the Lewd Sophia: Jewish Traditions in Gnostic Revolt', in B. Layton (ed.), *The Rediscovery of Gnosticism*, ii. *Sethian Gnosticism* (Leiden: Brill, 1981), 689–712 and E. A. Fischer-Mueller, 'Yaldabaoth: The Gnostic Female Principle in its Fallenness', *Novum Testamentum*, 32 (1990), 79–95.

[44] See Logan, *Gnostic Truth and Christian Heresy*, 129–42.

[45] 'It was probably because of his role as guardian of the deceased in the netherworld, and as an intermediate between the various deities, that he became associated with the Greek god Hermes in the Ptolemaic period'. See 'Thoth' in I. Shaw and P. Nicholson (eds.), *The British Museum Dictionary of Ancient Egypt* (London: British Museum Press, 1995), 288–9 (289).

[46] *Gospel of the Egyptians*, III.58.3–22 (*Nag Hammadi Library*, 214–15); *Apocryphon of John*, II.10.28–11.4 (*Nag Hammadi Library*, 110–11).

[47] *Gospel of Philip*, 56.7–9 (*Nag Hammadi Library*, 144).

[48] On this last point, see F. T. Fallon, 'The Gnostics: The Undominated Race', *Novum Testamentum*, 21 (1979), 271–88, and for general remarks on the topic, R. Bergmeier, ' "Königlosigkeit" als nachvalentinianisches Heilsprädikat', *Novum Testamentum*, 24 (1982), 316–39. There may also be a polemic here against the idea of Jesus as King, which is prominent in the New Testament.

[49] There is also a 'star' which 'led' the magi to Jesus in Matt. 2: 9.

[50] Mark 9: 2–8/Matt. 17: 1–8/Luke 9: 28–36.

[51] E. Pagels, 'Gospel Truth', *New York Times* (8 Apr. 2006).

[52] B. D. Ehrman, *The Lost Gospel of Judas Iscariot: A New Look at Betrayer and Betrayed* (New York: Oxford University Press, 2006), 98, 137.

[53] Krosney, *The Lost Gospel*, 277; Meyer, Introduction, 9.

[54] Ehrman, *The Lost Gospel of Judas Iscariot*, 98, 136.

[55] L. Painchaud, abstract of paper, 'À propos de la (re)découverte de l'*Évangile de Judas*' (presented to *Christian Apocryphal Texts for the New Millennium* Conference, Ottawa, Sept. 2006).

CHAPTER 5 THE CAINITES

[1] For Irenaeus as 'heresy hunter', see e.g. B. D. Ehrman, 'Christianity Turned on its Head: The Alternative Vision of the Gospel of Judas', in R. Kasser, M. Meyer, and G. Wurst, (eds.), *The Gospel of Judas* (Washington, DC: National Geographic, 2006), 77–120 (88); H. Krosney, *The Lost Gospel: The Quest for the Gospel of Judas Iscariot* (Washington, DC: National Geographic, 2006), 181.

[2] Ehrman, 'Christianity Turned on Its Head: The Alternative Vision of the Gospel of Judas' in Kasser, Meyer, and Wurst, *The Gospel of Judas*, 77–120 (89).

[3] For these quotations, see respectively A. Rousseau and L. Doutreleau, *Irénée de Lyon: Contre les hérésies* (10 vols.; Sources Chrétiennes; Paris: Cerf, 1965–82), IV.1.186; J. A. Robinson, 'The Armenian *Capitula* of Irenaeus *Adv. haereses* IV', *Journal of Theological Studies*, 32 (1931), 71–4 (74); B. Hemmerdinger, in Rousseau and Doutreleau, *Irénée de Lyon*, IV.1.42.

[4] See respectively Rousseau and Doutreleau, *Irénée de Lyon*, I.1.37 and 41.

[5] Gregor Wurst points this out in his essay in the National Geographic volume. See G. Wurst, 'Irenaeus of Lyon and the Gospel of Judas', in Kasser, Meyer, and Wurst, *The Gospel of Judas*, 121–35 (124). See also B. Pearson, 'Cain and the Cainites', in id., *Gnosticism, Judaism, and Egyptian Christianity* (Minneapolis, Minn.: Fortress, 1990), 95–107 (esp. 96).

[6] Wurst, 'Irenaeus of Lyon and the Gospel of Judas', 127–8.

[7] This point is made by both S. Emmel and R. Kasser, according to their comments quoted in Krosney, *The Lost Gospel*, 198.

[8] J. M. Robinson, *The Secrets of Judas: The Story of the Misunderstood Judas and his Lost Gospel* (New York: HarperSanFrancisco, 2006), 53. See also Krosney, *The Lost Gospel*, 3–4.

[9] Wurst, 'Irenaeus of Lyon and the Gospel of Judas', 128.

[10] Ibid., 130.

[11] Ibid., 131–2: it is surely not 'clear' as Wurst claims (p. 131).

[12] Neither has the situation gone away. Hugh Pyper's fascinating essay 'Modern Gospels of Judas: Canon and Betrayal' (*Literature and Theology*, 15 (2001), 111–22) surveys a number of twentieth-century works, including: Ernest Sutherland Bates, *The Gospel of Judas* (1929); Henryk Panas, *The Gospel According to Judas* (1973); Michael Dickinson, *The Lost Testament of Judas Iscariot* (1994). A search on amazon.com reveals two other books entitled the *Gospel According to Judas*, as well as Simon Mawer's novel *The Gospel of Judas* (2005) and now Jeffrey Archer's *The Gospel According to Judas by Benjamin Iscariot* (2007).

[13] F. Williams (trans. and ed.), *The Panarion of Epiphanius of Salamis*, 2 vols. (Nag Hammadi Studies, vols. 35–6; Leiden: Brill, 1987, 1994), i, p. xvi.

[14] Williams, *The Panarion of Epiphanius*, 1. xvii. The summary is at *Panarion*, Anacephalaeosis, III. 38.

[15] The picture of these Cainites is reasonably consistent throughout the fathers, and the positions attributed to them (such as the association with Judas) are too specific for them to be easily dismissed as a literary fabrication. Contrast the view in B. Pearson, 'Cain and the Cainites', in id., *Gnosticism, Judaism, and Egyptian Christianity* (Minneapolis, Minn.: Fortress, 1990), 95–107 (esp. 105–7).

CHAPTER 6 REWRITING HISTORY

[1] H. Krosney, *The Lost Gospel: The Quest for the Gospel of Judas Iscariot* (Washington, DC: National Geographic, 2006), 283.

[2] Ibid., 275.

[3] G. Wurst, 'Irenaeus of Lyon and the Gospel of Judas', in R. Kasser, M. Meyer, G. Wurst (eds.) (with additional commentary by B. D. Ehrman), *The Gospel of Judas* (Washington, DC: National

Geographic, 2006), 121–35 (132–3). The parallels are between Acts 1: 21–6 and the top of p. 36 in the codex.

[4] Luke hedges his bets and follows Mark's spelling at Luke 6: 16 and the alternative at 22: 3.

[5] This phrase does occur in the OT and additionally in the NT in Heb. 11: 28.

[6] On the other side, there are a few minor instances of language more reminiscent of Mark and Luke. For example, in the reference to the Jewish leaders fearing the people/crowds, the *Gospel of Judas* has— with Luke—'people', rather than Matt.'s 'crowds'. And Mark and Luke (but not Matt.) refer to a 'guest room' (as the place where the Passover will be celebrated), and this crops up on the final page of the *Gospel of Judas*, although with a different function.

[7] E. Massaux, *The Influence of the Gospel of Saint Matthew on Christian Literature before Saint Irenaeus*, iii. *The Apologists and the Didache* (Macon, Ga.: Mercer University Press, 1993), 187.

[8] C. M. Tuckett, *Nag Hammadi and the Gospel Tradition: Synoptic Tradition in the Nag Hammadi Library* (Edinburgh: T. & T. Clark, 1986), 149.

[9] According to early church tradition, the last of the Gospels was written by 'John' when he was an old man of 80 or 90 years of age.

[10] See most recently, R. J. Bauckham, *Jesus and the Eyewitnesses: The Gospels as Eyewitness Testimony* (Grand Rapids, Mich.: Eerdmans, 2006), 52.

[11] See, for example, D. E. Nineham, *Saint Mark* (Pelican New Testament Commentaries; Harmondsworth: Penguin, 1969), 431.

[12] B. D. Ehrman, 'Christianity Turned on Its Head: The Alternative Vision of the Gospel of Judas', in Kasser, Meyer, and Wurst, *The Gospel of Judas*, 77–120 (117–18). See the similar viewpoint in id., *Lost Christianities: The Battles for Scripture and the Faiths We Never Knew* (New York: Oxford University Press, 2003), 248.

[13] Ehrman, 'Christianity Turned on Its Head', 81.

[14] E. Pagels, *The Gnostic Gospels* (New York: Random House, 1979), pp. xxii–xxiii.

[15] <http://www.worldchristiandatabase.org/wcd/about/denominat ionlist.asp>.

[16] The National Geographic's time-line puts the composition of Matt., Mark, Luke, and John in the period 65–95 CE, which probably reflects the scholarly consensus (Krosney, *The Lost Gospel*, p. x).

[17] Ehrman, 'Christianity Turned on Its Head', 80.

CHAPTER 7 BRAVE NEW WORLD

[1] H. Krosney, *The Lost Gospel: The Quest for the Gospel of Judas Iscariot* (Washington, DC: National Geographic, 2006), 275.

[2] Clement of Alexandria, *Excerpta ex Theodoto*, 78.2.

[3] On Gnostic ritual, see most recently A. H. B. Logan, *The Gnostics: Identifying an Early Christian Cult* (London/New York: T. & T. Clark, 2006), 76–88.

[4] Matt. 1: 22–3; 2: 5–6, 15, 17–18, 23.

[5] Mark 14: 21 = Matt. 26: 24 ≈ Luke 22: 22.

[6] J. M. Robinson, *The Secrets of Judas: The Story of the Misunderstood Judas and his Lost Gospel* (New York: HarperSanFrancisco, 2006), 39–40.

[7] M. Meyer, Introduction, in R. Kasser, M. Meyer, G. Wurst (eds.) (with additional commentary by B. D. Ehrman), *The Gospel of Judas* (Washington, DC: National Geographic, 2006), 1–16 (9–10).

[8] Krosney, *The Lost Gospel*, 295.

[9] Ibid., 308.

[10] Plato, *Gorgias*, 485D; Epictetus, *Discourses*, II.12.17. I owe these references to C. K. Barrett, *The Acts of the Apostles*, ii. *Introduction and Commentary on Acts XV–XXVIII* (International Critical Commentary; London/ New York: T. & T. Clark, 1998), 1169.

[11] Mark 4: 10–12; Matt. 13: 10–13; Luke 8: 9–10.

[12] *Gospel of Mary*, 17: 7–18: 14. See James M. Robinson (ed.), *The Nag Hammadi Library* (New York: HarperCollins, 1990), 526–7.

[13] According to one interpretation of the first epistle of John, 'docetic christology' is condemned in these terms: 'This is how you can recognize the Spirit of God: Every spirit that acknowledges that Jesus Christ has come in the flesh is from God, but every spirit that does not acknowledge Jesus is not from God.' (1 John 4: 2–3).

[14] Krosney, *The Lost Gospel*, 278.

[15] Ibid., 286.

[16] As quoted ibid., 196

[17] The quotation is from Meyer, Introduction, 9.

Select Bibliography

A. ANCIENT SOURCES IN ENGLISH TRANSLATION

Holy Bible: New Revised Standard Version (New York: American Bible Society, 1989).

Apostolic Fathers
Holmes, M. W. (trans. and ed.), *The Apostolic Fathers in English* (Grand Rapids, Mich.: Baker Academic, 2006).

Church Fathers
Roberts, A. and Donaldson, J. (eds.), *The Ante-Nicene Fathers*, i. *The Apostolic Fathers—Justin—Irenaeus* (Edinburgh: T. & T. Clark, 1989) (includes Irenaeus' *Against Heresies*).

———— (eds.), *The Ante-Nicene Fathers*, iii. *Latin Christianity: Its Founder, Tertullian* (Edinburgh: T. & T. Clark, 1989) (includes Pseudo-Tertullian, *Against All Heresies*).

Williams, F. (trans. and ed.), *The Panarion of Epiphanius of Salamis*, 2 vols. (Nag Hammadi Studies, 35–6; Leiden: Brill, 1987, 1994).

Gnostic Writings from Nag Hammadi
Robinson, James M. (ed.), *The Nag Hammadi Library* (New York: HarperCollins, 1990).

Other Apocryphal Gospels and Acts
Schneemelcher, W. (ed.), *New Testament Apocrypha*, i. *Gospels and Related Writings*, ii. *Writings Relating to the Apostles; Apocalypses*

Select Bibliography

and Related Subjects (Louisville, Ky.: Westminster John Knox, 1991).

B. Works Cited

Barrett, C. K., *The Acts of the Apostles*, ii. *Introduction and Commentary on Acts XV–XXVIII* (International Critical Commentary; London/New York: T. & T. Clark, 1998).

Barth, K., *The Church Dogmatics*, II/2: *The Doctrine of God* (Edinburgh: T. & T. Clark, 1957).

Baumgarten, J. M., 'The Duodecimal Courts of Qumran, the Apocalypse, and the Sanhedrin', *Journal of Biblical Literature*, 95 (1976), 145–71.

Berger, K., 'Zur Diskussion über die Herkunft von I Kor. II.9', *New Testament Studies*, 24 (1978), 270–83.

Bergmeier, R., ' "Königlosigkeit" als nachvalentinianisches Heilsprädikat', *Novum Testamentum*, 24 (1982), 316–39.

Brown, D., *The Da Vinci Code* (London: Corgi, 2003, 2004).

Cockburn, A., 'The Judas Gospel', *National Geographic*, 209/9 (May 2006), 78–95.

Crum, W. E., *A Coptic Dictionary* (Oxford: Clarendon Press, 1939).

Dahl, N. A., 'The Arrogant Archon and the Lewd Sophia: Jewish Traditions in Gnostic Revolt', in B. Layton (ed.), *The Rediscovery of Gnosticism*, ii. *Sethian Gnosticism* (Leiden: Brill, 1981), 689–712.

Davies, W. D. and Allison, D. C., *The Gospel according to St Matthew*, iii. *Matthew XIX–XXVIII* (International Critical Commentary; Edinburgh: T. & T. Clark, 1997).

Eco, U., *The Name of the Rose* (London: Secker and Warburg, 1983).

Ehrman, B. D., *Lost Christianities: The Battles for Scripture and the Faiths We Never Knew* (New York: Oxford University Press, 2003).

_____ *The Lost Gospel of Judas Iscariot: A New Look at Betrayer and Betrayed* (New York: Oxford University Press, 2006).

Select Bibliography

Evans, C. A., 'Appendix 2: What Should We Think about the *Gospel of Judas?*', in id., *Fabricating Jesus: How Modern Scholars Distort the Gospels* (Downers Grove, Ill.: Intervarsity Press, 2006), 240–5.

Fallon, F. T., 'The Gnostics: The Undominated Race', *Novum Testamentum*, 21 (1979), 271–88.

Fischer-Mueller, E. A., 'Yaldabaoth: The Gnostic Female Principle in its Fallenness', *Novum Testamentum*, 32 (1990), 79–95.

Hancock, C. L., 'Negative Theology in Gnosticism and Neoplatonism', in R. T. Wallis (ed.), *Neoplatonism and Gnosticism* (Albany, NY: SUNY Press, 1992), 167–86.

Horbury, W., 'The Twelve and the Phylarchs', in id., *Messianism among Jews and Christians: Biblical and Historical Studies* (London/New York: Continuum, 2003), 157–88.

Kasser, R., Meyer, M., and Wurst, G. (eds.) (with additional commentary by B. D. Ehrman), *The Gospel of Judas* (Washington, DC: National Geographic, 2006). (Also available in French, German, and Spanish trans.)

Klassen, W., *Judas: Betrayer or Friend of Jesus?* (London: SCM Press, 1996).

Klauck, H.-J., *Judas—ein Jünger des Herrn* (Freiburg/Basle/Vienna: Herder, 1987).

Klijn, A. F. J., *Seth in Jewish, Christian and Gnostic Literature* (Leiden: Brill, 1977).

Krosney, H., *The Lost Gospel: The Quest for the Gospel of Judas Iscariot* (Washington, DC: National Geographic, 2006).

Layton, B. (ed.), *The Rediscovery of Gnosticism*, ii. *Sethian Gnosticism* (Leiden: Brill, 1981).

Layton, B., *A Coptic Grammar*, 2nd edn. (Wiesbaden: Harrassowitz Verlag, 2004).

Logan, A. H. B., *Gnostic Truth and Christian Heresy: A Study in the History of Gnosticism* (Edinburgh: T. & T. Clark, 1996).

——— *The Gnostics: Identifying an Early Christian Cult* (London/New York: T. & T. Clark, 2006).

Select Bibliography

Maccoby, H., *Judas Iscariot and the Myth of Jewish Evil* (New York: The Free Press, 1992).

Markschies, C., *Valentinus Gnosticus? Untersuchungen zur valentinianischen Gnosis mit einem Kommentar zu den Fragmenten Valentins* (Tübingen: Mohr, 1992).

Massaux, E., *The Influence of the Gospel of Saint Matthew on Christian Literature before Saint Irenaeus*, iii. *The Apologists and the Didache* (Macon, Ga.: Mercer University Press, 1993). (First pub. 1950 in French.)

Pagels, E., 'Gospel Truth', *New York Times* (8 Apr. 2006).

_____ *The Gnostic Gospels* (New York: Random House, 1979).

Pearson, B., 'Cain and the Cainites', in id., *Gnosticism, Judaism, and Egyptian Christianity* (Minneapolis, Minn.: Fortress, 1990), 95–107.

Plisch, U.-K., 'Das Judasevangelium', in id., *Was nicht in der Bibel Steht: Apokryphe Schriften des frühen Christentums* (Stuttgart: Deutsche Bibelgesellschaft, 2006), 165–77.

_____ 'Das Evangelium des Judas', *Zeitschrift für antikes Christentum*, 10 (2006), 5–14.

Pyper, H., 'Modern Gospels of Judas: Canon and Betrayal', *Literature and Theology*, 15 (2001), 111–22.

Reade, J., 'Alexander the Great and the Hanging Gardens of Babylon', *Iraq*, 62 (2000), 195–217.

Robinson, J. A., 'The Armenian *Capitula* of Irenaeus *Adv. haereses* IV', *Journal of Theological Studies*, 32 (1931), 71–4.

Robinson, J. M., *The Secrets of Judas: The Story of the Misunderstood Judas and his Lost Gospel* (New York: HarperSanFrancisco, 2006).

Rousseau, A. and Doutreleau, L., *Irénée de Lyon: Contre les hérésies* (10 vols.; Sources Chrétiennes; Paris: Cerf, 1965–82).

Schwarz, G., *Jesus und Judas: Aramaistische Untersuchungen zur Jesus-Judas-Überlieferung der Evangelien und der Apostelgeschichte* (Stuttgart: Kohlhammer, 1988).

Select Bibliography

Shaw, I. and Nicholson, P. (eds.), *The British Museum Dictionary of Ancient Egypt* (London: British Museum Press, 1995).

Stead, G. C., 'The Valentinian Myth of Sophia', *Journal of Theological Studies*, 20 (1969), 75–104.

Thiselton, A. C., *The First Epistle to the Corinthians* (Grand Rapids, Mich.: Eerdmans, 2000).

Tuckett, C. M., *Nag Hammadi and the Gospel Tradition: Synoptic Tradition in the Nag Hammadi Library* (Edinburgh: T. & T. Clark, 1986).

―――― 'Paul and Jesus Tradition. The Evidence of 1 Corinthians 2: 9 and Gospel of Thomas 17', in T. J. Burke (ed.), *Paul and the Corinthians: Studies on a Community in Conflict: Essays in Honour of Margaret Thrall* (Leiden: Brill, 2003), 55–73.

Turner, J. D., 'Time and History in Sethian Gnosticism', in Hans-Gebhard Bethge, Stephen Emmel, K. L. King, and I. Schletterer (eds.), *For the Children, Perfect Instruction. Studies in Honor of Hans-Martin Schenke* (Nag Hammadi and Manichaean Studies, 54; Leiden/Boston: Brill, 2002), 203–14.

van der Toorn, K. and van der Horst, P. W., 'Nimrod before and after the Bible', *Harvard Theological Review*, 83 (1990), 1–29.

Vogler, W., *Judas Iskarioth: Untersuchungen zu Tradition und Redaktion von Texten des Neuen Testaments und ausserkanonischer Schriften* (Berlin: Evangelischer Verlagsanstalt, 1983).

Wright, N. T., *Judas and the Gospel of Jesus: A Christian Response* (Grand Rapids, Mich./ London: Baker/SPCK 2006).

This list includes the major treatments in print on the *Gospel of Judas* published in 2006. The most significant publication in 2007 has been R. Kasser and G. Wurst, eds. *The Gospel of Judas: Critical Edition* (Washington, D.C.: National Geographic, 2007), which contains the Coptic text on which the translation above is based.

Index of Authors and Select Topics

Index of Authors and Select Topics

Index of Authors and Select Topics

Index of Authors and Select Topics

Index of Authors and Select Topics

Index of Authors and Select Topics